THE
GOLFERS
REFERENCE
DICTIONARY
ILLUSTRATED

CLASSIC GOLF COLLECTION

SCHAEFER'S PUBLISHING
P.O. Box 5544
Dearborn, Michigan
48128 5544

THE GOLFERS REFERENCE
DICTIONARY ILLUSTRATED

WRITTEN BY: DUNCAN SWIFT

PUBLISHED BY: SCHAEFER'S PUBLISHING
P.O. BOX 5544
DEARBORN, MI.
48128-5544
E-MAIL: schaed@idt.net

ARTWORK BY: DAVID ANTHONY
SAVELLE GRAHAM
DONNA NYE

EDITING: MADELAIN HOPE
NICKLAUS COPELAND
JASMINE KINGFISHER

FIRST EDITION 1999
ISBN: 0-9658132-1-5
LIBRARY OF CONGRESS CATALOG CARD NUMBER: 98-89215

THE GOLFERS REFERENCE
DICTIONARY ILLUSTRATED

TABLE OF CONTENTS

INTRODUCTION

THE GOLFERS REFERENCE DICTIONARY ILLUSTRATED is dedicated to people everywhere who have a yearning to learn everything they can about this wonderful game called golf. Words transform a person who knows nothing or very little about golf into a person who knows some things about golf until he or she becomes a golf aficionado.

Words are the indispensable vehicle of human existence. It is the means by which human beings communicate with each other and when they understand each other. They now create the ability to function together as a group or community. Certainly, in the absence of words, the complex structure of individuals and human society would be utterly impossible.

The effectiveness of human beings, is largely dependent on the clarity, accuracy and efficiency with which words are used to bring about understanding for the ultimate goal of communication. Whether people are in the classroom, at the job, on the playground or on the golf course the importance of people's words is paramount.

THE GOLFERS REFERENCE DICTIONARY ILLUSTRATED is proud to present this collection of golf definitions and expressions, with the exclusive purpose of teaching people about the game of golf. In doing so, we arrive closer to our ultimate goal of transforming a world of people into a world of golf aficionados.

Duncan Swift

**HAPPY READING, HAPPY LEARNING
AND HAPPINESS ALWAYS ON AND OFF THE GOLF COURSE.**

THE
GOLFERS
REFERENCE

DICTIONARY
ILLUSTRATED

ABNORMAL LIE:
Ball resting in casual water, ground under repair, and/ or a hole made by a burrowing animal. You may take a drop without penalty.

ACAPULCO:
Golf game with partners playing for low ball. Both partners drive from each tee and select one ball to play. Alternating shots thereafter until holed.

ACCELERATED:
1. To increase the speed of the clubhead.
2. The clubhead being accelerated throughout the hitting area.

ACCELERATION / TO ACCELERATE:
The speed of your downswing past the belt line as you are swinging through the ball. The increase changes in velocity of the hands, arms and clubhead from the beginning of the downswing.

ACCEPTABLE SCORE:
A gross score made in an 18-hole round or by combining the scores of two nine-hole rounds. In addition, when a golfer plays 13 or more holes during a round, the score is recorded for handicapping purposes.

ACE:
A shot that goes from the tee into the cup in one stroke. A hole scored in one stroke. Also called **HOLE IN ONE**.

ACTION

ACED:
To play a hole in one stroke.

ACTION:
The movement and/or spin placed on the ball. Also called **BACKSPIN, BITE, VAMPIRE, REVERSE SPIN, ENGLISH, BICUSPID** or **OVER-BITE**.

ACTIVE SEASON:
The active season is the time, during which golfers' scores are accepted for handicap purposes. The golf association determines **THE ACTIVE SEASON**.

ADDRESS:
The position of a player's body in relation to the ball just before impact. The position or stance of the player at the ball before the swing. Also called **SET UP**.

ADDRESSING THE BALL:

The action of the golfer when he positions or stands at the ball and soles the club behind the ball before swinging. In a hazard, you have addressed the ball once you have taken your stance. When addressing the ball in a hazard, you cannot sole your club on the ground.

ADDRESSING THE
BALL

ADJUSTED GROSS SCORE (AGS):

The "Adjusted Gross Score" is a golfer's gross score adjusted under **USGA HANDICAP SYSTEM** procedure for unfinished holes, conceded strokes and holes not played. Applying the **EQUITABLE STROKE CONTROL METHOD** to the golfer's actual gross score. This reduces the number of strokes taken over par.

ADJUSTMENT/ TO ADJUST:

1. <u>Scoring</u> - A designated number of strokes are used on each hole according to an individual handicap. When a player exceeds this number, the score is adjusted to the maximum number allowed.
2. <u>Posture</u> - To realign the position of the hands, body, club or swing.

ADVICE:

Any counsel or suggestion that could influence a player on how to play, choose a club, or make a stroke. Only partners and caddies may be consulted without penalty. Information about a golf rule or some thing that is general knowledge; for example, the position of hazards or the flagstick, is not considered advice. According to the Rules of Golf, giving or asking advice from anyone, except a partner or a cad die is not allowed. A transgression of this rule in match play results in the loss of one hole; its violation in medal play results in the loss of one stroke.

AERATE:

Pulling out round cylinders of grass and soil from fairways and greens to supply the turf with oxygen.

AFRAID OF THE DARK:

1. A putt that does not fall into the cup.
2. A golfer who refuses to play a round of golf in the late evening.

AGGREGATE SCORE:

Refers to a score made over more than one round of play, or by two or more players playing as partners. Also called **AGGREGATE**.

AGGRESSIVE:

Taking the first step in attacking the hole. Not playing safely but playing offensively and confidently.

AIM:
> The alignment of the body and clubface in the direction of a chosen target. Also called **ALIGNMENT**.

AIM LINE:
> The imaginary line running from the ball to the target. Also called **TARGET LINE, LINE** and **LINE OF INTENDED FLIGHT**.

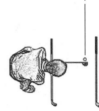

AIRMAIL:
> A ball that flies over the putting green.

AIM LINE

AIR BALL:
> A swing that misses the ball completely. Also called **AIR SHOT, WHIFF, FAN, SILENT SHOT** and **NO NOISE ON THAT ONE**.

AIR SHOT:
> Missing the ball completely. Also called **AIR BALL, WHIFF, FAN, SILENT SHOT** and **NO NOISE ON THAT ONE**.

ALBATROSS:
> Playing a hole in three strokes under par. This is a British term.
> Example: A par five completed in two shots or a hole in one on a par four would also be an albatross. Also called a **DOUBLE EAGLE.**

ALIGNMENT:
> How the golfer aims his body and the golf club at the intended line of flight. Also called **AIM**.

ALL SQUARE:
> A term used when the score is tied in match play.

AMATEUR:
> Someone who plays for fun and not for money. Someone who is not a professional.

AMATEUR SIDE:
> The area below the hole on a sloping green. Also called the **LOW SIDE**.

AMATEUR SIDE

AMERICAN BALL:
> The golf ball as officially specified by the USGA having a diameter not less than 1.68 inches and a weight not more than 1.62 ounces.

AMPHITHEATER:
> Putting green situated in a bowl-shaped hollow.

ANGLE OF APPROACH:
1. The steepness of the swinging path which influences the trajectory and distance of a ball. Also called **ANGLE OF ATTACK**.
2. The angle taken to approach the round, hole and/or the green.

ANGLE OF ATTACK:
The angle at which the clubhead approaches the ball on the downswing and through the ball at impact. Also called **ANGLE OF APPROACH**.

ANXIETY:
Uneasy thoughts or fears over the possibility of missing your shot or other misfortunes.

APPROACH:
A shot made onto or towards the green. Usually refers to a medium or short iron shot.

APPROACHING:
Playing or attempting to play a ball onto the putting green.

APPROACH

APPROACH PUTT:
A long putt taken and not holed, but close enough to make the next putt a certainty. Also called a **LAG PUTT**.

APPROACH SHOT:
Any shot made toward or on the green.

APRON:
The area around the perimeter of the green. They usually cut the grass shorter than the fairway but not as short as the green. Also called the **FRINGE, COLLAR** and **FROG HAIR**.

ARC:
The path taken by the clubhead throughout the swing. The route of the clubhead during the swing.

ARCHED WRIST:
The left wrist at the top of the golf swing which will produce a closed clubface.

ARCHITECT:
A designer of golf courses.

ARC

ARCHITECTURE:
The theory and practice of golf course design; the nature and design characteristics of any particular golf course.

ARMY GOLF:
Slang expression for the inconsistent golfer who hits the ball to the right-left and left-right. Also called **MILITARY GOLF** and **SPRAY HITTER**.

ARNIE:
When a player misses the fairway off the tee, hits the green in regulation, and makes par or better. This is named after Arnold Palmer. Also called **ARNIE AWFUL.**

AS THEY FALL:
Refers to players recieving handicaps strokes on the lowest handicap holes.

ASSISTANT:
Trainee professional golfer or aide.

ATTACK:
To play aggressively with purpose.

ATTEND THE FLAG:
To hold or remove the flagstick as your partners putt.

ATTESTED:
A scorecard signed in agreement.

ATTEND THE FLAG

AUTHORIZED:
A person, business or organization that is recognized by the **R&A, PGA, LPGA** or the **USGA**.

AUTHORIZED GOLF ASSOCIATION:
A USGA licensed golf association that issues USGA Handicap Indexes as well as USGA Course and Slope Ratings.

AUTOMATIC PRESS:
The same as the press, except a player does not have a choice as to when he adds the press. The press is automatically added anytime a player is two holes down on any bet. Also called **AUTOMATICS.**

AWAY:
The ball farthest from the hole when more than one golfer is playing. Usually the person who is away takes their shot first.

AWAY SHEET:
The document used for posting your scores when playing a golf course other than your own.

AXIS:
A straight line around which a body rotates. There are several axes in the golf swing. The one most frequently referred to is the spine, around which the upper body rotates.

BACK:
1. The teeing ground moved the farthest distance from the hole, used by the better players, so that the hole is played at its longest distance. Also called **BACK TEE, CHAMPIONSHIP TEE** and **TIGER TEES**.
2. Designating the last nine holes of an eighteen-hole course. Also called **BACK NINE, SECOND NINE, LAST NINE, IN NINE, BACK SIDE, BACK HOLES, IN, SECOND HALF, HOMEWARD NINE, LAST HALF** or **INWARD HALF**.

BACKSPIN:
1. The spin on the ball caused by the loft of the clubface.
2. A reverse spin put on the ball to make it stop on the green or roll backward. It is the clockwise spinning action imparted on the ball by the face of the club. Also called an **ACTION, BITE, VAMPIRE, BICUSPID, JUICE** or **OVERBITE**.

BACKSTROKE:
The moving of the clubhead away from the ball to the top of the backswing. Also called **BACKSWING**.

BACKSWING:
The moving of the clubhead away from the ball to the top of the backswing. The backswing is a vital movement in the golf swing. It should be smooth, fluid and performed as one movement. Also called **BACKSTROKE**.

BACKSWING

BACK DOOR:
The rear of the hole. A ball that goes around the hole and drops into the cup from the backside is said to have "dropped in the back door."

BACK DOOR PUTT:
A putt that enters the cup from the rear of the cup. Also called the **TRADESMEN ENTRANCE**.

BACK HOLES:
Designating the last nine holes of an eighteen-hole course. Also called **BACK NINE, SECOND NINE, LAST NINE, IN NINE, BACK SIDE, BACK, IN, SECOND HALF, HOMEWARD NINE, LAST HALF** or **IN-WARD HALF**.

BACK LIP:
Edge of the bunker that is farthest from the green.

BACK MAKER:
The player with the lowest handicap in the group.

BACK NINE:
The last nine holes of an 18 hole course. Also called **SECOND NINE, LAST NINE, IN NINE, BACK SIDE, BACK HOLES, IN, SECOND HALF, HOMEWARD NINE, LAST HALF** or **INWARD HALF**.

BACK TEE:
The teeing ground located the farthest distance from the hole, used by the better players. Also called **BACK, PRO'S TEES, CHAMPIONSHIP TEE** and **TIGER TEES**.

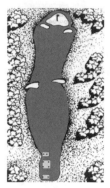
BACK TEE

BAFF:
1. An old Scottish term meaning to hit or graze the ground before the ball. To strike the ground with the club before hitting the ball.
2. A slap in the face.
3. A blow made by something soft.

BAFFIE (BAFFY):
A short wooden club with a laid back clubface for lofting shots. An obsolete wooden club equivalent to the **FOUR** or **FIVE WOOD**. Developed from the **BAFFING-SPOON** no longer in use. Also called the **FOUR WOOD**.

BAFFING SPOON:
A wooden club no longer in production that was the shortest, stiffest and most lofted club in the set. It was used for approach shots, considered equal to the modern wedge. Also called **BAFFY SPOON**.

BAFFLE:
Nickname for the **FIVE WOOD**.

BAG:
A receptacle for carrying clubs made of canvas, leather, or synthetic material, having a shoulder strap and a handle, and often containing separate compartments for balls, tees, gloves. Also called a **CADDIE BAG, GOLF BAG** or **SUNDAY BAG**.

BAG

BAGFUL:
1. Used as a comparison for the whole array of a player's clubs and equipment.
2. A repertoire of a player's shots. Also called a **SHOT MAKER**.

BAG RAT:
Referring to the caddie.

BAIL OUT:

1. To avoid a hazard in one area by hitting the ball into another area. Hitting the shot well to the right to avoid hazards on the left. Also called **LAYING UP**.
2. Holing a long putt to avoid losing a hole.
3. Improved play from a poorly started hole.

BAIL OUT

BAIL OUT AREA:
Places on the course where the golfer can safely play his shot to avoid trouble.

BALANCE:
Address position at which equilibrium is obtained; can also apply to a well-positioned follow- through. A state we should try to achieve during the golf swing despite being put "off balance" by movement. Equilibrium in a static position at address.

BALATA:
A hard resilient sap from a tropical tree, used to make covers for golf balls. Derived from the gum of the bully or balata tree (Manilkara bidentata) of northeastern South America and the West Indies.

BALATA BALL:
With liquid or rubber-centered cores. Designed for faster swing speeds. Has soft pliable cover that offers more control, but is easier to cut, as it magnifies imperfections in the swing. Favored by the professionals.

BALLS

BALL:
The hard and resilient spherical projectile used in golf. The round object which we try to hit into a hole. The ball we use today is usually made in either two or three pieces. Two-piece balls consist of a core and a cover. Three-piece balls, which are the more traditional, consist of a core, rubber windings around the core, and a cover. Golf ball cores are usually liquid or rubber. Covers are typically made from Surlyn or Balata. A golf ball is usually 1.68 inches in diameter and weighes 1.62 ounces.

BALL AT REST:
A ball that is not moving and completely stops its motion.

BALL DEEMED TO MOVE:
A ball that has moved from its original stopping position and comes to rest in another place.

BALL FLIGHT LAWS:
The physical relationship between clubhead path and angle that influences the ball's flight, identical for every golfer and for every swing.

BALL HOLED:
A ball that is entirely below the lip of the cup.

BALL IN PLAY:
A ball struck by a player and staying within the boundaries of the golf course. When a player makes a stroke on the teeing ground, the ball becomes "in play" and remains so until holed out, unless the ball is lost, out of bounds, or lifted. In addition, if another ball is substituted under a rule, that ball becomes the ball in play.

BALL LOST:
The rules allow you five minutes to find a lost ball. If after that time it is still not found, you must put another ball into play. Also called **LOST BALL**.

BALL MAKER:
A manufacture of golf balls.

BALL MARKERS

BALL MARK:
An indentation made by a ball after it hits the green or fairway. Also called a **PITCH MARK**.

BALL MARKER:
A small round object used to indicate the exact position of the ball on the green. A small object or coin is used as a ball marker.

BALL POSITION:
The position of the ball in relation to the feet in the setup position.

BALL RETRIEVER:
Long pole with a scoop on the end used to collect balls from water hazards and other trouble areas.

BALL RETRIEVER

BALL ROUNDNESS GAUGE:
A device used to measure exactly how "round" a golf ball is. This helps to ensure precision in the equipment used in the game.

BALL-TO-TARGET LINE:
An imaginary line extending through the golf ball
to the intended target.

BALL WASHER:
A device used for cleaning golf balls.

BANK SHOT

BANK SHOT:
A shot around the green deliberately played into a bank or hill to deaden
the speed while still allowing the ball to bound forward. Also called
the **BUMP AND RUN**.

BANANA BALL:
A shot that severely curves from the left to the right and its arc looks
like a banana. Refers to an extreme slice.

BAP HEADED:
The head of a wooden club used in late 19th and early 20th centuries,
mostly round and flattish in shape, compared with the long-nosed woods
of earlier times.

BARBER:
A talkative golfer to the point of annoyance.

BARKIE:
When a golfer hits a tree with the ball and still manages to par the hole.
Makes no difference where on the tree the ball hits. Also called a
WOODIE.

BARRANCA:
Typically, a rocky or heavily wooded deep ravine sometimes played as
a hazard.

BARRACUDA:
A golf game played on the putting green. Also called
SNAKE.

BASEBALL GRIP:
To hold the club with all ten fingers. Not recom-
mended for use on the golf club. Also called the **TEN
FINGER GRIP**.

BASEBALL GRIP

BASICS:
An essential part; fundamental or rule. The forming of a base or fundamentals.

BE RIGHT:
1. Expression used when the player hopes that his or her ball has landed to the right of the target.
2. Expression used by the golfer when they hope that they have selected the proper club for the distance needed.
3. Expression used by the golfer to his or her caddie.

BE THE BALL:
Expression used to stay focused with the shot at hand.

BEACH:
A reference to a sand trap or bunker on a golf course. Also called a **SAND TRAP, BUNKER** or **TRAP**.

BEACH ONE:
To land a shot into a sand trap or bunker.

BEACH

BEHAVIORAL PRACTICE:
The process of learning the game in a series of steps, from the simplest skill to the most difficult.

BEHIND THE BALL:
The body position at address and during the swing in which the head and torso are to the right of an imaginary line drawn vertically from the ball.

BELLIED SHOT:
A shot hit slightly better than a topped ball. It gets the ball in the air, but does not travel high or far. Also called **THIN SHOT** or **BLADED**.

BELT ONE:
To hit a ball well while applying extra power.

BEND:
1. The curve placed on a shot created by sidespin.
2. To cause a shot to curve by using sidespin imparted at impact.
3. A bending of the upper body forward from the hips, just enough to allow your arms to hang freely.

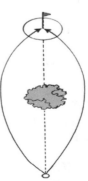

BEND ONE:
To hook or slice a shot.

BEND ONE

BENT GRASS:
1. The species of grass most often found on the green. Used on Northern golf courses. Any grass of the genus Agrostis, native to moist northern parts of Eurasia and North America, selectively bred in many varieties for use on golf courses. It is healthy and resilient and can be cut very short.
2. Scottish word, meaning a clump of turf on the links.

BERMUDA GRASS:
A species of grass found on the green when bent grass will not grow there. Used in the Southern golf courses. A grass, Cynodon dactylon, native to southern Europe, widely introduced in warm parts of the world.

BEST BALL:
1. A match in which one golfer plays against the better ball of two players or best ball of three players.
2. A competition where two or more players form a team. The best net score per team on each hole is recorded on the scorecard. Each team's score is determined, on a hole by hole basis, by taking the best individual score posted by a member of the team. Best ball is adaptable to match and medal play golf. Also called **BETTER BALL**.

BEST BALL MATCH:
A match in which a single player competes against the better ball of two others.

BEST SHOT:
A team competition where each member of the team plays a shot, the best placed ball is then chosen and all other players of the same team play their next shot from that position. This procedure is repeated for each shot until a player holes out. Normally used with stroke play, best shot can be adapted to any form of competition.

BETTER BALL MATCH:
A match in which two partners play as a team and only the better score counts for either team. Also called **BEST BALL** or **FOUR BALL**.

BICUSPID:
A spin that makes the ball tend to stop rather than roll when it lands. Also called **VAMPIRE, BITE, OVERBITE** or **BACKSPIN**.

BICUSPID

BIG BERTHA:
A modern driver with an oversized head.

BINDWEED:
A species of grass found on the golf course.

BINGO, BANGO, BONGO:
Golf game. Three points are awarded on each hole. One point - first on the green, one point - closest to the hole and one point- first in the hole. Also called **BINGLE, BANGLE, BUNGLE**.

BIRD:
1. Slang term meaning anyone or anything excellent or wonderful.
2. Used by golfers for a fine shot, implied that it "flew like a bird."
3. An obsolete term meaning a long, impressive shot.

BIRD'S NEST:
A ball that is resting in a cuppy lie in the deep rough.

BIRDIE:
Any hole played out in one stroke under the regulated par is called a birdie.

BIRDIED:
Playing a hole one stroke under the regulated par.

BIRD'S NEST

BIRDIE ABLE:
The possibility of shooting one under par on the hole you are playing.

BISQUE:
A handicap stroke given by one player to another. The receiver may choose when to use it.

BISQUE BOGEY:
To use bisques in bogey competition or match play. Bisques are strokes that can be taken where a player chooses, instead of at an allotted time.

BITE:
How well the ball stops upon hitting the putting green. A spin that makes the ball stop rather than roll when it lands. Also called **VAMPIRE, BICUSPID, OVERBITE** or **BACKSPIN**.

BITE YOU BALL:
Expression used when the golfer wants the ball to stop after landing on the green. Also called **BITE, CHEW, GROW TEETH** and **BITE YOU**.

BITE YOU BALL

BLADE:
1. A term used to describe a type of shot where the upper part of the ball is hit causing it to travel with low trajectory or run along the ground. Also called **TOPPING** or **BLADING**.
2. Slang term referring to the hitting part of an iron club.
3. Slang term referring to the **BLADE PUTTER**.

BLADED:
Shot one that has a low line trajectory because of having been struck on the lower portion of the clubface on or above the equator of the ball. Also called **BLADE SHOT**.

BLADES MAN:
A description of a person who is an excellent putter.

BLADE PUTTER:
A type of putter with an iron head with a basic form.

BLADED

BLADE SHOT:
To strike the ball above its center causing it to skip and bounce along the ground rather than rise through the air. Also called a **THIN SHOT** or **BLADED**.

BLAST:
1. An aggressive bunker shot that displaces a lot of sand. Also called an **EXPLOSION**.
2. The material carried with the ball when it is hit out of a sand bunker.

BLASTER:
1. An old term for a broad-soled bunker club. Also called a **SAND WEDGE**.
2. A nickname for the one wood. Also called a **DRIVER** or **ONE WOOD**.

BLIND:
A hole or shot where you cannot see your target.

BLADE PUTTER

BLIND BOGEY:
Competition in which player estimates before starting what handicap will be needed to put his net score between 70 and 80, and thus qualify him for a blind drawing of a winning number in that range.

BLIND DRAW:
Selecting a partner from a hat.

BLIND GREEN:
A blind hole is one where the player cannot see the putting green as he or she approaches it.

BLIND HOLE:
A blind hole is one where the player cannot see the putting green from the teeing ground. Also called a **DOG LEG**.

BLIND HOLE TOURNAMENT:
Format in which scores are culled from any of the 18 holes.

BLIND HOLE

BLIND SHOT:
When you cannot see the spot where you want the ball to land.

BLOCK:
To prevent or delay the rotation of the arms, body, wrists or club in the forward swing. Resulting in a shot starting and remaining right of the intended flight.

BLOCK AND FOLD:
Folding or collapsing the left arm at the elbow in the forward swing so that it is bent, pointing away from the side of the body. Considered a swing fault; however, it can be used effectively to stop clubface rotation such as in a bunker shot, pitch shot or putt. Also called **CHICKEN WING**.

BLOCK SHOT:
To play a shot by delaying the rotation of the wrists during the swing. Normally, this causes the ball to veer to the right for a right-handed golfer or slice.

BLOW IT:
To suffer a sudden collapse of good play, typically when under pressure. Also called **CHOKE**, **BLOW**, **BLOW UP**, **CRACK**, **LOST IT** or **BLEW IT**.

BLUEGRASS:
A cool weather grass with moderate size blades that can thrive in a variety of climates. Mostly found in Kentucky.

BLUE DARTER:
A shot that is hit solidly and low into the wind. Also called **WINDCHEATER** and similar to the **PUNCH SHOT**.

BOBBING:
Lowering then raising, or raising then lowering the swing path during the course of the swing.

BODY COIL:
The full turn away from the ball made by the hips and shoulders; the source of power in the golf swing. Also called **COIL** and **POWER COIL**.

BODY ENGLISH:
The leaning or twisting movements that a player makes to persuade the ball to go in a desired direction.

BODY MOTION:
Used to describe the rotational movement of the body during the golf swing.

BOG GRASS:
A species of grass found on the golf course.

BODY ENGLISH

BOGEY:
1. One stroke more than the designated par.
2. The number of strokes an average player should take to each hole. This imaginary player is known as "Colonel Bogey" and plays a good game.

BOGEY COMPETITION:
A match play competition in which the golfer plays a hole-by-hole match against bogey. The player receives three quarters of his handicap and takes those in the form of strokes from par according to the stroke index.

BOGEY GOLFER:
The USGA defines a "bogey golfer" as having a USGA Handicap Index of 17.5 to 22.4 for men, and 21.5 to 26.4 for women.

BOGEY RATING:
A bogey rating is the evaluation of the playing difficulty of a course for the bogey golfer under normal course and weather conditions.

BOGEY TRAIN:
A series of consecutive bogies by a golfer.

BOLD:
1. Refers to a shot played too strongly and passing the intended target.
2. To play aggressively.

BOLD SHOT:
A firmly played approach shot to a well-protected pin in a difficult position.

BOMB:
1. To hit a very long shot.
2. To lose a hole or a round.

BOLD SHOT

BONE:
A piece of horn, wood or hard composition placed in the sole of the clubhead at its front edge to protect it from damage.

BONG:
Golf game. Types of shots made on the course are given a number value. The player with the highest total loses.

BORING:
Refers to a low shot that holds its course through the wind.

BORON:
An extremely strong and expensive metal put in the tips of graphite shafts for added strength.

BORROW:
The amount of distance you have to aim to the right or left when putting to allow for slope of the green to bring the ball back to the hole. The amount of compensation in aim taken on the putting green when the player has to deal with a side slope, gravity, grain or the wind's effect on the ball.

BOSS OF THE MOSS:
A player who is proficient on the putting surface.

BOLT:
To make a putt with a hard and fast moving ball. Also called **SLAM DUNK** and **DRAIN**.

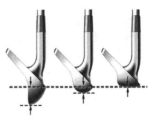

BOUNCE

BOUNCE:
1. The angle between the leading edge and the highest point on the sole of an iron club, most often referred to when discussing sand irons.
2. The reaction of the ball after landing or hitting the ground, tree, cart path, etc. Also called **BREAK**.

BOUNDARY:
The edge of the golf course that defines the area of play.

BOWKER:
Refers to a shot that appears to be terrible and then hits an object and bounces back into play. It is pronounced "BOUGHKUR."

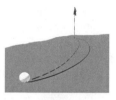

BREAK

BRAMBLE:
A small molded bump on some types of golf balls (**GUTTA PERCHA**) intended to give aerodynamic properties like the dimples used on the today golf balls.

BRASSIE (BRASSY):
A number two wooden club. Also called the **TWO WOOD**.

BREAK:
1. To make less than a specified score. Such as when a player breaks 70.
2. The way the ball will roll or bounce after hitting the ground or some object. Also called **BOUNCE**.
3. The sideways slope of the green. The curved line a ball travels on the ground because of slope, grain or wind. A putts sideways curve as it rolls on the green. Also called **BORROW**.
4. Refers to the bending at a joint, like a wrist or elbow.

BREAKFAST BALL:
To hit a second shot from the first tee. Also called **MULLIGAN**.

BREAK CLUB:
Obsolete term meaning an object or obstruction that might break a club.

BREAK THE WRIST:
To bend the wrists back during a swing. Also called **COCK** or **HINGE**.

BREAK THE WRIST

BRITISH BALL:
The type of ball specified by the Royal and Ancient Golf Club of St. Andrews. Now used mainly in amateur play. The diameter is 1.62 inches, and its weight is 1.62 ounces.

BRITISH OPEN:
National championship run by the Royal and Ancient Golf Club of St. Andrews. Known to the Britains as the "The Open" because it was the first European Open.

BROAD FOCUS:
    The ability to gather information on the big picture, such as wind, lie, hazards and any other information that may affect the shot.

BROGUE:
    Origin: Scottish - A tool, consisting of an iron prong set in a wooden crosspiece, that was used for ramming boiled feathers into the leather cover of a feathery golf ball.

BROOM:
    Expression used to describe a putting stroke.

BUBBLE SHAFT:
    Modern club shaft design.

BUGGY

BUGGY:
    Colloquial term for a motorized golf cart. A powered cart used to transport golfer and equipment around the course. Also called a **GOLF CART**.

BULGE:
    The curve across the face of a wooden club.

BULGER:
    A wooden club with a slightly convex face used mainly on the driver.

BULLRUSHES:
    A species of grass found on the golf course.

BULL'S EYE PUTTER

BULL'S EYE PUTTER:
    A rocker type putter which is a variation of the blade putter. Sometimes called a **CENTER SHAFTED PUTTER**.

BUMP AND RUN:
    1. A shot around the green deliberately played into a bank or hill to deaden the speed while still allowing the ball to bound forward. Also called the **BANK SHOT**.
    2. A low shot played from off the green that lands short of the putting surface, bounces and rolls towards the hole. Similar to the **RUN UP SHOT**.

BUNKER:
    A hazard filled with sand. A depression in the fairway, rough or near the green, either grass or filled with sand. Also called a **BEACH, SAND, SANDBOX, SAND TRAP** or **TRAP**.

BUNKER CARE:
Golfing etiquette requires that footprints and other marks should be raked before leaving the bunker.

BUNT:
To hit an intentional short shot that is kept low to avoid the wind.

BURIED BALL:
Half of a ball below the surface of sand in a bunker. Also called **BURIED LIE**.

BURN:
The Scottish term for a stream or creek.

BURIED BALL

BURNER:
A tee shot that is hit low, hard and skimming the ground. Also called **BLUE DARTER** and **WORM BURNER**.

BUTT:
The top end of the clubshaft and grip.

BUTTERFLY LANDING:
When the ball lands softly on the green. Also called **A BUTTERFLY WITH SORE FEET**.

BUTTON HOOK:
A putt that rolls around the cup before coming out of the front edge of the cup. Also called a **HORSESHOE**.

BUZZARD:
A score of two strokes over par on a hole. Also called a **DOUBLE BOGEY**.

BYE:
1. A term used in tournaments. The player who has the "bye" is allowed to advance to the next round without playing an opponent.
2. In match play, it is the hole or holes still left to play if the match is won before the 18 th hole. Also called **BYE HOLES**.

BYE HOLES:
In match play, unplayed holes after the match has been won.

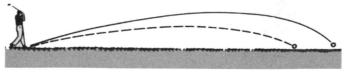

BURNER

CABBAGE:
1. Deep, heavy and thick rough.
2. Money won from a bet.

CADDIE (CADDY):
The person who carries a player's clubs and often assists the player in accordance with the rules.

CADDIE BAG (CADDY BAG):
A golf bag.

CADDIE CAR:
A golf cart or car.

CADDIE CART:
A two-wheeled trolley for carrying clubs.

CADDIE BAG

CADDIE MASTER (CADDY MASTER):
The person in charge of the caddies. The person who manages the caddies.

CALAMITY JANE:
Bobby Jones' favorite wooden shafted putter. It was a hickory-shafted blade putter.

CALCUTTA:
A format for tournament play. Players are paired normally by blind draw and auctioned off to the highest bidder.

CALLAWAY HANDICAP SYSTEM:
A handicap system that applies to 18-hole regulation courses only. This particular system allows for the handicapping of players who do not have an established handicap, a system generally associated with large outings. In this system a golfer's handicap is determined after the completion of the round. The gross score of the golfer determines the handicap adjustment by eliminating a worst hole or worst holes and subtracting the adjustment from the player's gross score.

CAMBUCA
A later derivative of paganica, a popular pastime around the 12th century AD in Britain. It was played in very much the same way as modern golf, but played with a wooden ball.

CAN:
1. To hole a putt.
2. The actual cup itself.

Hole	COURSE RATING MEN	WOMEN	1	2	3	4	5	6	7	8	9	Out
Red	64.5	66.0	304	78	208	226	333	304	400	75	287	2,405
White	67.5	72.9	313	138	474	252	367	352	450	113	330	2,789
Blue	70.1		346	170	490	283	387	372	498	142	350	3,038
Gold	73.4		390	192	515	310	441	438	515	152	366	3,322
	Men's Handicap		12	16	6	10	2	8	4	18	14	
Par			4	4	5	4	4	4	5	4	4	36
	Ladies Handicap		7	15	5	13	3	9	1	17	11	

CARD

CARD:
The player's official score card. Also called **SCORECARD**.

CARPET:
A slang term referring to the putting surface or even the fairway.

CARRY:
1. The distance between a ball's takeoff and landing.
2. The distance the ball travels in the air.
3. To carry clubs; serve as a caddie.
4. To play clear over a hazard or obstacle.

CARRY OVER:
A bet that is carried over from one hole to another.

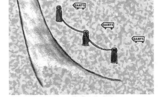

CART

CART:
A motorized or non-motorized vehicle used to transport a golfer's clubs. A two-wheeled trolley on which a golf bag can be fitted and hauled around a course. Some are electrically powered. Also called **TWO WHEELER, GOLF CART, CADDIE CAR, CADDIE CART, TROLLEY** and **BUGGY**.

CART FEE:
Fee charged for use of the cart on the course.

CART GIRL:
The young lady who operates the beer or refreshment cart. Also called **BEER LADY** and **NICE LADY**.

CART GOLF:
When two golfers riding in the same golf cart hit their balls consistently in the same direction.

CART PATH

CART PATH:
A cart path is the path upon which motorized golf carts travel. These paths are usually located parallel to fairways.

CASTING:

A premature release of cocked wrists on the forward swing which causes the clubhead to arrive at the ball out of sequence, ahead of the hands and arms. Also called **HITTING FROM THE TOP** or **EARLY RELEASE**.

CASUAL LIE:

A ball lying in water which has accumulated temporarily. A free lift is granted by the rules of golf.

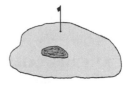

CASUAL LIE

CASUAL WATER:

Casual water is a temporary accumulation of water on the course. If your ball lands in casual water you may remove it and drop it without penalty. Water hazards are not considered casual water.

CAUSE AND EFFECT:

A teaching term where the instructor finds a chain reaction in the golf swing with a set-up or swing movement being the cause and the fault being the effect.

CAVITY-BACKED CLUB DESIGN:

Refers to the distribution of weight on an iron. Designed to provide a larger sweet spot by weighting the club on the outside or perimeter of the clubhead. Useful for golfers who often miss the center of the clubface. Also called **PERIMETER WEIGHTED**.

CELLOPHANE BRIDGE:

A term used when the golf ball rolls over the cup without dropping into the hole.

CENTER OF GRAVITY (BODY):

The point in the body somewhere in the pelvic region usually near the navel where the upper mass, lower mass, right and left sides all balance.

CELLOPHANE BRIDGE

CENTER OF ROTATION:

The axis around which the body winds and unwinds, usually thought of as the spine.

CENTER PUTT:

A putt that goes directly into the center of the cup. Also called **CENTER CUT**.

CENTERED SHAFTED PUTTER:
A putter in which the shaft is joined to the center of the head. A common example is the **BULL'S EYE PUTTER**.

CENTRIFUGAL FORCE:
The power created from within, which is forced outward, created by the body rotating during the golf swing.

CENTRIPETAL FORCE:
The action of rotating the body, that tends to move mass away from center. The force one feels in the swing that pulls the clubhead outward (backswing) and downward (downswing). The force that tends to move things toward the center, around which they are turning. Gravitation is an example.

CENTERED
SHAFTED PUTTER

CHAMPIONSHIP:
A tournament sponsored by a recognized golfing organization such as the USGA or the Royal and Ancient Golf Club of St. Andrews in which golfers compete for a trophy or title plus prizes or monetary reward if the golfer is a professional. Championship tournaments are generally held on an annual basis.

CHAMPIONSHIP TEE:
The teeing ground located the farthest distance from the hole, used by the better players. Also called **BACK TEE** and **TIGER TEES**.

CHANGING THE SPINE ANGLE:
Elevating the central area in the body somewhere between the top of the spine and center of the neck around which rotation takes place. What the novice frequently refers to as looking up and which results in a swing that is too high. Also called **RAISED SWING CENTER**.

CHARGE:
1. To surge from behind and display superior play.
2. To roll a putt towards the hole with a bold and powerful stroke. To play or putt aggressively.
3. A spectacular rush of superior play, especially by a player who has been losing.

CHARTING THE COURSE:
Calculating the distance needed on each hole and plotting out a shot plan for the round.

CHARTING THE COURSE

CHAPMEN SYSTEM:
A form of competition in which two players play with two balls each, then hole out with the best ball.

CHEW:
Expression used when the player wants the ball to stop after landing on the green. Also called **BITE, GROW TEETH, BITE YOU** and **BITE YOU BALL**.

CHECKING UP:
When the ball stops quickly upon hitting the green because of the backspin. Opposite of **RELEASE**.

CHI-CHI:
When a player misses the fairway and green and still makes par or better in regulation. Named after Chi Chi Rodriguez.

CHICKEN WING:
A fault on the downswing in which the left arm folds or collapses at the elbow in the forward swing so that it is bent, pointing away from the side of the body. Considered a swing fault; however, it can be used effectively to stop clubface rotation such as in a bunker shot, pitch shot or putt. Also called **BLOCK AND FOLD.**

CHILI-DIP:
A mis-hit. The clubhead hits the ground well be- fore it hits the ball. The clubhead digs into the turf and moves the ball just a few feet. Also called **HORMEL** and **LAY THE SOD OVER IT**.

CHILI-DIP

CHIP AND RUN:
A stroke similar to the **PITCH AND RUN**, but usually made using a club with less loft. A golfer would use a chip and run stroke from just short of the green, playing the shot in almost the same way as he or she would putt.

CHIP IN:
A holed chip.

CHIP OFF:
A method used to determine the winner of a tied hole.

CHIP SHOT:
With no hazards in the way. A short and low tra- jectory approach shot to the green. Known to have a bit of a roll on this shot. Used just short of the green and playing the shot is similar to putting.

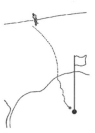

CHIP AND RUN

CHIPPER:
A club designed only for chip shots. This club is most effective from the fringe.

CHIPPING:
The act of shooting any of the variety of short shots played around the green.

CHIPPING

CHIPPING IRON:
An iron club used for making a short, low-trajectory shot, most often from near the green. Most chips are done with the five and six irons.

CHOKE:
To miss a golf shot under pressure. Also called **BLOW, BLOW IT, BLEW IT, CRACK** and **LOST IT**.

CHOKE DOWN:
To grip down further on the handle of the club intentionally to prevent full power on the swing.

CHOKE UP:
To grip the club handle higher than normal.

CHOKE DOWN

CHOLE:
An ancient Flemish golf like game played in the 14th century. The ball is made of beechwood and is struck with clubs forged from rigid shafts with iron heads.

CHOP:
To hit the ball with a hacking motion.

CH'UI WAN
Literally meaning "hitting ball", the first reference to it can be traced back to 943 A.D in China. The game is believed to have involved hitting a ball into a series of pits. It was apparently the favorite sport of the Emperor Huizong. One theory suggests that it was imported into Europe by tradesmen doing business in the Far East and it eventually evolved into golf.

CHUMP:
An easy opponent.

CHUNK:
Occurs when the club hits the ground behind the ball before hitting the ball. This action causes a high or low shot and loss of distance. Also called a **FAT SHOT**.

CHUNKING:
A shot in which the clubhead strikes the ground before striking the ball, causing a partial hit, decreasing the distance the ball travels. Also called **STUBBING, SCUFFING, DUNCHING, SCLAFFING, HEAVY** and **FAT**.

CHUNKING

CINCO:
Golf game where five points are possible on each hole. The scoring is two points for low score, one point for closest to the pin, one point for natural birdie, and one point for sandy par. Also called **FIVE POINTS**.

CLEARING THE LEFT SIDE:
Turning the hips to the left of the target so the arms may follow in sequence. Also called **CLEAR**.

CLEATS:
The plastics spikes on the bottom of golfing shoes. Many golf courses are making it manditory to wear cleats opposed to metal spikes.

CLEATS

CLEEK:
1. A nickname for the **FOUR WOOD**.
2. A nickname for the **ONE IRON**.
3. An old Scottish name for a shallow-faced iron. Originally, a cleek was the club with the least loft, except for the putter. The equivalent to the **TWO IRON** or a putting iron with loft.
4. Scottish word meaning, from hook, crook, walking stick with a hook.

CLEEKMAKER:
Person who hand-makes iron clubs.

CLICK:
1. The gratifying sensation of hitting the ball well and the sound it makes.
2. To come abruptly into top golfing form. Everything seem to click together.

CLOSE LIE:
Ball sitting directly on top of the ground with no grass supporting and lifting the ball off the ground.

CLOSE LIE

CLOSED:
The relationship between the direction of the stance and the clubface.

CLOSED CLUBFACE:

1. A position where a golfer turns the clubface inward in order to minimize a slice. Also called a **CLOSED FACE, HOODED** or **SHUT**.
2. The clubface is pointing to the left of your target at address or impact.

CLOSED CLUBFACE (HOODED)

CLOSED CLUBFACE SWING PATH:

Whenever the angle formed by the leading edge of the clubface is less than 90 degrees to the tangent of the swing arc.

CLOSED FACE GRIP:

An exaggerated clockwise rotational positioning of the hands when placed on the grip, i.e., left hand more on top of the shaft, right hand more under. Also called a **STRONG GRIP**.

CLOSED CLUBFACE

CLOSED STANCE:

The moving of your right foot back of the intended line of flight for the right-handed golfer. Encourages a hook.

CLOSED TO OPEN:

A description of the dynamics of the clubhead when the player hoods and closes the clubface in the backswing pointing more to the ground then reverses it to open coming through pointing more to the sky. Also called **SHUT TO OPEN**.

CLOSED STANCE

CLUB:

1. The instruments used to hit the golf ball. The first golf clubs are assumed to have been made of wood. Club shafts were made of hazel, hickory, and ash while blackthorn, beech, apple, and pear were used for the heads. Modern club heads are made of laminated plastic and even lightweight aluminum. Steel shafts have been replaced by more flexible graphite, titanium, boron, and other materials. Also called **GOLF CLUB**.
2. An organization of at least ten individual members operating under bylaw and having committees whose responsibility it is to supervise golf activities and maintain the integrity of the USGA Handicap System. Also called **GOLF CLUB**.

CLUBBING A PLAYER:

To advise a partner which club to use for a particular shot which is against the rules. Also called **CLUBBING**.

CLUBFACE ALIGNMENT:
The direction in which the clubhead is aimed at address relative to the target line.

CLUBFACE:
The portion or area of a clubhead that makes contact with the ball.

CLUBHEAD:
The portion of the golf club that comes in contact with the ball.

CLUBHEAD ANGLE:
The direction in which the clubface points at impact; relative to the target.

CLUBFACE ALIGNMENT

CLUBHEAD COVERS:
Mittens slipped over the heads of the woods to keep them dry.

CLUBHEAD SPEED:
The force with which the club swings through the ball, measured in miles per hour.

CLUBHOUSE:
A golf course facility used to house locker rooms, meeting rooms, restaurants, bars, and similar accommodations. The clubhouse is frequently used for relaxation after a round of golf.

CLUBHEAD COVERS

CLUBHOUSE LAWYER:
A self-appointed caller or arbiter of the rules.

CLUB LENGTH:
The distance from the end of the grip to the sole of the head.

CLUB LOFT:
Club loft is the angle at which the clubface is set to lift the ball into the air. Also called **LOFT**.

CLUB SHAFT:
The long, thin part of the club connecting the grip and club head. Also called the **SHAFT**.

CLUB WEIGHT:
The overall weight of the club.

CLUB WEIGHT

COCKED WRISTS:
To bend the wrists backwards in the backswing. Also called **BREAK THE WRISTS, HINGED** and **COCKED**.

COCKED WRISTS, BOWED:
A position at the top of the swing in which the wrists have cocked but the back of the left hand has moved farther away from the top of the left arm (falmar-flexion), palm toward the underside of the forearm.

COCKED WRISTS

COCKED WRISTS, CUPPED:
A position at the top of the swing in which the wrists have cocked and the back of the left hand has moved closer to the topside of the forearm. Also called **DORSAL-FLEXION**.

COCKED WRISTS, IN PLANE:
A position in which the wrists have cocked and the back of the left wrist is flat in line with the forearm, and the right wrist is parallel to the left wrist. Also called **RADIAL-FLEXION**.

CUPPED
DORSAL-FLEXION

COEFFICIENT OF RESTITUTION:
The relationship of the clubhead speed at impact to the velocity of the ball after it has been struck. A measure affected by the clubface and ball material.

COIL:
Another word used to describe the movement of the body during the backswing. Also called **BODY COIL**.

COLLAR:
The grass around the edge of the green or sand trap.

COLONEL BOGEY:
An imaginary player who always shoots one over par on every hole.

COMEBACK PUTT:
The follow-up putt after the previous putt has rolled past the hole.

COMEBACK SHOT:
The shot you make after you have overshot the hole.

COIL

COME OFF THE BALL:
To lift the body prematurely during the swing.

COME OUT:
To play out of a bunker.

COME OVER THE TOP:
To steepen the plane or arc of the swing during the downswing and throw the clubhead outside the target line prior to impact.

COME UP EMPTY:
To lose a hole or miss a carefully planned shot.

COME OUT

COMMITTEE:
The people in charge of a competition and of the course during a competition. They are responsible for enforcing the USGA Handicap System as well as peer reviews.

COMMON CLUB:
Obsolete term meaning the **DRIVER** or **ONE WOOD**.

COMPETITION SCRATCH SCORE:
The number of strokes needed to complete a course under competition conditions. The number of strokes cannot exceed three strokes above the Standard Scratch Score. The CSS is calculated by using all the scores recorded in the competition.

COMPRESSION:
1. The flattening of the ball against the clubface.
2. This is how tight the core of the golf ball is wound. The tighter the core the higher the compression.

CONCEDE:
To give an opponent a putt, hole or match.

COMPETITOR:
An opposing player or team in a stroke or match play competition.

COMPRESSION

CONCENTRATION:
Keeping intact the same routine and protecting yourself from disturbances. Focusing the mind on the shot at hand in a positive manner with close attention to detail.

CONDOR:
A hole played in four under par. Also called a **TRIPLE EAGLE**.

CONFIDENCE:
A firm belief and trust in one's self. Certain in one's abilities. Faith in your golfing ability to make shots.

CONNECTION:
Maintaining the various moving parts in the appropriate relationship to one another before or during the swing to produce harmonious movement. Also referred to as **TIMING**.

CONSERVATION OF ANGULAR MOMENTUM (COAM):
A law of physics which allows the player to produce large amounts of kinetic energy. As the body shifts its weight and turns toward the target in the forward swing, the mass (arms and club) is pulled away from the center into an extended position by centrifugal force. By temporarily resisting that pull as well as the temptation to assist the hit by releasing too early, one maintains the angle formed between the club shaft and the left arm and conserves the energy until a more advantageous moment. Also called **DELAYED HIT, LATE HIT, CONNECTION, LAG LOADING, THE KEYSTONE, COAM** and **GOOD TIMING**.

CONTROL SHOT:
A shot that is played with less than full power.

CONSECUTIVE NINE-HOLE SCORES:
To combine the score of two nine-hole rounds played consecutively within seven days to arrive at a score suitable for handicap adjusment. When determining handicap differential, the golfer must use the course rating for each of the nine holes. A golfer will record a score for handicap purposes if he plays 13 or more holes. To do this, add the number of strokes played to the sum of the par for any unplayed holes and finally, apply the number of handicap strokes for the un-played holes.

COP:
1. The **RANGER** or **STARTER** on the golf course.
2. Obsolete term meaning a knoll or bank regarded as a hazard or obstacle. Also called a **COP BUNKER**.

COP BUNKER:
Obsolete term meaning a knoll or bank re-garded as a hazard or obstacle. Also called a **COP**.

COUPLE

COUPLE:
Two players playing together in a stroke competition.

COURSE:

The area within, where playing golf is permitted. The term usually assumes a 9-hole or 18-hole facility with each hole, including a tee, fairway, and putting green. Also called **GOLF COURSE** and **LINKS**.

COURSE HANDICAP:

A player receives a certain amount of handicap strokes, depending on the course and individual tees, in order to increase the chance of 0-handicap golf. The USGA determines a Course Handicap by applying the golfer's USGA Handicap Index to either a Course Handicap Table or a Course Handicap Formula, and then expressing the golfer's Course Handicap as a whole number.

COURSE HANDICAP CONVERSION CHART:

A chart for each individual hole that uses your Handicap Index to decide your Playing or Course Handicap for the course you are playing.

COURSE HANDICAP TABLE:

A chart that converts a USGA Handicap Index to a Course Handicap based on the USGA Slope Rating for the set of tees played. A chart for each individual hole that uses your Handicap Index to decide your Playing or Course Handicap for the course you are playing.

COURSE RATING:

A rating assigned to the difficulty of a course in comparison to other courses, measured by the USGA.

COURTESY:

Polite behavior and thoughtfulness for your fellow people on the golf course. Type of conduct specifically mandated by the rules.

CORE:

The center of the golf ball.

CORE

COW PASTURE:

A poorly maintained golf course.

CRACK:

1. Referring to a first class or champion caliber player.
2. To hit a good drive or long shot.
3. The cutting or cracking of the outside layer of the golf ball, usually caused by the leading edge of the club tearing into the cover. Also called a **SMILE** or **CUT**.
4. To suffer a sudden collapse of good play, as in to choke.

CRACK

CRENSHAW:
An expression used when a player chips from off the green and holes it for par or better. Also called **WATSON**.

CROQUET STYLE:
A putting stance in which the player stands facing the hole using the putter in a fashion similar to playing croquet. Originally he stood astride the line, but now, by rule, must stand beside it. Sometimes refered to as **SIDESADDLE**.

CROQUET STYLE

CROSS BUNKER:
A large bunker that is situated across the fairway.

CROSS HANDED GRIP:
Gripping the golf club with the left hand below the right hand. A grip style usually employed in putting, where the left hand is placed be low the right on the club's grip.

CROSS HAZARD:
A hazard situated astride a fairway.

CROSS THE MARGIN:
Used to describe the point where a ball crosses the boundary line of a hazard.

CROSS HANDED
GRIP

CROSSING THE LINE:
Manipulating the club so it comes from the target line to the inside during the downswing, resulting in a shot that flies left to right.

CROSSWIND:
Wind that is blowing from either side.

CUP:
1. The hole where the flagstick is placed when on the green. The cup is actually the plastic container that sits in the bottom of the hole.
2. Obsolete term meaning a small deep depression or hole on the course.
3. To hole the ball or to put one in.

CUPPED LIE:
When the ball is sitting in a cup like depression in the ground. Also called a **CUPPY LIE**.

CUP

CUPPED WRIST:
A position the left wrist can get into at the top of the backswing which usually results in an open clubface.

CUPPY:
A deep and enclosed lie. Also called **CUPPIE.**

CURTIS CUP:
The competition between amateur women golfers of the United States and Britain.

CUT

CUT:
1. A cut is a type of spin on the ball that causes it to travel to the right for right-handed golfers, causing the ball to slice. Also called **SLICE.**
2. The point where the field of players in competitions is reduced.
3. The height of the different grasses on the golf courses.
4. A tear or similar damage to a golf ball. Also known as a **SMILE** or **CRACK.**

CUTOFF:
The score, for the first two rounds of a four-round tournament, which competitors must equal or beat to remain in the tournament for the last two rounds.

CUT ONE IN:
To play a precision approach or pitch shot with backspin to a cup lying in a guarded position.

CUT SHOT:
Used to clear hazards between you and the green. There is hardly any roll on this shot. It stops almost at once when it hits the putting green.

CUT SPIN:
The clockwise rotation of the ball that causes it to fly in left to right for the right-handed golfer.

CUT SHOT

DANCE FLOOR:
Refers to the putting green. Also called **GREEN, PUTTING SURFACE, PUTTING GREEN** and **STAGE**.

DAWN PATROL:
Those players who tee off early in the morning.

DEAD:
1. A ball that lies so close to the hole, it is virtually impossible to miss it and it is given by the opposing player or team in match play. It is counted as one stroke if the putt is conceded. Also a **GIMMIE** and **DEAD BALL**.
2. Describes a shot that hits the green and stops immediately.
3. Describes a position from which escaping is impossible. Also called **DEAD LIE**.
4. A ball when it is pitched to the green falls dead with no roll. Also called **DEAD DROP**.

DEAD BALL:
A ball is dead when there is no doubt that it will be sunk on the next shot. Also called **DEAD**.

DEAD LIE:
No possible way to take the shot. Also called **DEAD**.

DEAD

DEAD WRISTS:
A term used mostly for shots on and around the green where the wrists do not cock back or release through; rather, they stay fixed and unhinged.

DECELERATION:
1. Negative changes in the velocity of a moving object.
2. In golf, it refers usually to decreasing clubhead speed. It is a major error when occurring before impact. Also called **NEGATIVE ACCELERATION** and **QUITTING**.

DEEP FACED:
Having a clubface that is relatively thick from top to bottom. A clubhead that has a higher than normal face height.

DEEP STUFF

DEEP STUFF:
Grass left to grow so that off-line shots are made more difficult. Very tall and thick grass. Also called **ROUGH** and **HIGH AND HEAVY**.

DEFENDER:
Golf game played in threesomes. The object is to win as many points as possible.

DELAYED HIT:
Retaining the wrist cock until the last possible moment in the down-swing, just before impact. Also called **HITTING LATE** or **LATE HIT**.

DELIVERY PLANE:
A plane which is parallel to the shaft plane, but slightly above, on which the clubshaft and right forearm should be prior to impact.

DEPTH CHARGE:
Ball shot into the water. Also called **POND BALL** and **WATER BALL**.

DEUCE:
A hole made in two shots.

DEW SWEEPER:
A shot that roles along the ground a few feet.

DIE INTO THE CUP

DIE:
A putt or a putted ball that stops rolling short of the hole.

DIE INTO THE CUP:
Putting the ball so that it falls into the cup as it is on its last roll of momentum. Also called **DIE IT INTO THE HOLE**.

DIGGER:
A golfer who takes a divot on all of his or her iron shots.

DIMPLE:
Depression or indentation in the surface of a golf ball. Dimples cause the ball to maintain a true steady flight.

DIMPLE PATTERNS:
The dimple size and arrangement on the ball. Dimples affect the trajectory and flight of the ball. Generally, small deep dimples will produce low trajectory shots, and large shallow dimples produce higher shots.

DISC GOLF:
Played like golf but using a Frisbee instead of a ball and clubs. Also called **FRISBEE GOLF**.

DISTANCE:
The length of yardage received on a shot.

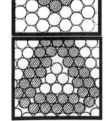

DIMPLE PATTERNS

DIVOT:

1. A piece of turf taken out of the ground by the clubhead after making contact with the ball. Good players will deliberately take a divot on their shot in order to impart more backspin on the ball to make it stop quickly on the green.
2. The cavity left by a divot.

DIVOT FIXER:

A tool used to repair ball marks or pitch marks on the green. Also called a **PITCH REPAIR TOOL** and **DIVOT TOOL**.

DIVOT FIXER

DIVOT PATTERN:

The divot pattern gives the indication of the swing path, angle of attack and the angle of the club at and through impact.

DOG IT:

To play poorly under pressure.

DOG LEG:

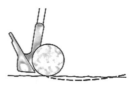

Any hole that has the green situated at an angle from the fairway and is often hidden from the tee. A hole that is laid out with a sharp bend between the tee and the putting surface.

DIVOT

DOG LICENSE:

Slang expression for 7/6 results in match play. Derived from seven shillings and six pence once being the cost of a dog license.

DOG TRACK:

A poorly maintained golf course.

DORMIE (DORMY):

In match play a player is said to be **DORMIE** when he cannot lose. When a player or team is leading by a margin that makes loss impossible.

DORSAL FLEXION:

This is one of the four basic wrist movements. It is considered a disastrous position because it causes the club face to open up too much at the top of the backswing.

DOUBLE BOGEY:

A hole played two over the regulated par.

DORSAL FLEXION

Example: A par four played in six shots would be a double bogey.

DOUBLE BUNKERS:
Two bunkers across from one another.

DOUBLE CHEN:
Hitting the ball twice on the same shot. Also called **DOUBLE HIT**.

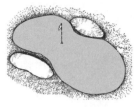

DOUBLE BUNKERS

DOUBLE D:
When the driver is used to hit off the fairway after it has been hit off the tee. Also called **DOUBLED DRIVER**.

DOUBLE DIP:
Occurs in a **FOUR BALL MATCH**, when you and your partner both make birdies on the same hole.

DOUBLE EAGLE:
A score of three under par on a hole. Also called an **ALBATROSS**.

DOUBLE SANDIES:
When a player takes two shots from the bunker and still makes par or better.

DOUBLE SNAKIE:
To four putt on the putting surface.

DOWNHILLER

DOWN:
1. In match play, down refers to the number of holes a golfer is behind his or her opponent.
2. In stroke play, the term refers to the number of strokes by which a golfer trails an opponent.
3. To sink a putt.
4. Playing with a sad or discouraged heart.

DOWNER:
1. An individual golfer who depresses other golfers.
2. When something depressing happens to a golfer.

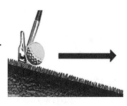

DOWNHILL LIE

DOWNHILLER:
A downhill shot or putt.

DOWNHILL LIE:
A downhill lie occurs when the ball is on a downward slope, with the slant towards the target. When your right foot is higher than your left foot when you address the ball.

DOWNSWING:
It is the swinging down at the ball after having paused at the top of the backswing. Keeping the clubhead in the proper position is important.

DOWNWIND:
When the wind is blowing at your back and you are facing towards the hole.

DOWN AND DIRTY:
To play the ball as it lies. Never moving the ball into a better hitting position.

DOWN THE ROAD:
1. When the ball is hit and bounces off the cart path.
2. Failing to qualify for the next round of play in a tournament.

DQ'D:
Disqualified.

DRAIN:
To sink a putt.

DRAG:
1. An aerodynamic force that resists the forward motion of an object. It influences clubhead speed and ball flight.
2. A golf shot played that has additional backspin.

DRAW

DRAW:
1. The pairing of golfers for match play.
2. The flight of the ball that curves from right to left.

DRAW SPIN:
The counterclockwise rotation of the ball, which causes it to fly right to left for the right-handed golfer.

DRAW SHOT:
Playing a controlled hook shot with the ball traveling to the right before coming in left towards its intended line of flight. The flight of the ball is the result of a counterclockwise spin imparted on the ball at impact.

DRESSING THE GREEN:
The process of placing a layer of sand and organic material on the green to smooth the surface.

DRIBBLE:
A shot that travels only a few feet after being hit.

DRILL:
Exercises and movement designed to ingrain swing changes in a golfer's body and mind.

DRINK:
Any body of water.

DRILL
LEFT ARM

DRIVE:
A ball hit from the teeing ground. The ball is usually teed up.

DRIVER:
Refers to the **ONE WOOD**. It is the most powerful club in the bag.

DRIVE AND PITCH:
The type of hole on which the green can be reached
with a drive and a pitch.

DRIVE FOR SHOW AND PUTT FOR DOUGH:
A golfers expression indicating that the money is
won on the putting green.

DRIVE THE GREEN:
When your drive finishes on the putting surface.

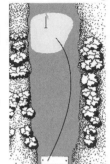

DRIVE THE GREEN

DRIVING IRON:
Most often a long iron such as a one or two iron. Also called the **ONE
IRON** or **CLEEK**.

DRIVING MASHIE:
An iron club, no longer in use, having less loft than a mashie-iron,
used for driving and for long shots to the green.

DRIVING PUTTER:
A straight-faced wooden club, no longer in use, that was used for driving low shots, especially against the wind.

DRIVING RANGE:
A place where you can go to practice hitting golf balls.

DROP:
The act of replacing the ball back into play after a player retrieves it
from an unplayable area such as out of bounds or a water hazard or
from ground under repair. Formerly made from over the player's shoulder, today a drop is made by the player stretching his or her arm out
lateral to or in front of himself / herself and releasing the ball from shoulder height.

DROP AREA:
Designated area where balls are dropped and played.

DROP KICK:
The clubhead striking the ground then bouncing into
the ball. Also called **CHILI DIP, DUBBED SHOT**
and **DUB**.

DROP

DUB:
   1. A bad shot
   2. A bad player.

DUBBED SHOT:
   The clubhead striking the ground then bouncing into the ball. Also called **CHILI DIP**, **DROP KICK** and **DUB**.

DUBBER:
   A golfer who does not play well. Also called a **DUFFER** and **HACKER**.

DUCK:
   The reaction of the ball to veer suddenly downward.

DUCK HOOK:
   A shot that bends sharply to the left and downward of the target. Also called a **SMOTHERED HOOK, SNAP** or **SNAP HOOK**.

DUFF, DUFFED or DUFFING:
   Hitting the ball improperly.

DUFFER:
   This would refer to a clumsy or a bad golfer. Also called a **HACKER**.

DUNCH:
   1. Origin: from Scottish dunch "to knock, bump, nudge".
   2. To play the ball along the ground with a forceful jabbing or poking motion.

DUNCHING:
   A shot in which the clubhead strikes the ground before striking the ball, causing a partial hit, decreasing the distance the ball travels Also called **STUBBING, SCUFFING, CHUNKING, SCLAFFING, HEAVY** and **FAT**.

DUNK:
   1. To hit your ball into a water hazard.
   2. To hole a hard rolling putt.

DYING PUTT:
   A putt that dies just before the cup.

DUNCHING

DYNAMIC BALANCE:
   Transferring the focus of weight appropriately during the golf swing while maintaining body control. Also called **BALANCE**.

EAGLE:
> A hole played in two strokes under par.

EAGLED:
> The act of scoring two strokes less than par on a hole.

EARLY RELEASE:
> A premature release of cocked wrists on the forward swing which causes the clubhead to arrive at the ball out of sequence, ahead of the hands and arms. Also called **HITTING FROM THE TOP, CASTING, EARLY HIT** or **HITTING EARLY**.

ECLECTIC:
> A system of scoring that takes the best score for each hole from multiple days of play.

EEL GRASS:
> A species of grass found on the golf course.

EFFECTIVE LOFT:
> The actual loft of the clubface when it strikes the ball. The player's technique and the built-in loft can be varied, thus becoming an effective loft.

EIGHT IRON

EFFECTIVE PLAYING LENGTH:
> The measured length of the golf course adjusted by factors that make the course longer or shorter than it's measured length.

EGYPTIAN GRASS:
> Refers to a sand trap. Also called **BEACH, SAND, SAND BOX, SAND TRAP** and **TRAP**.

EIGHT IRON:
> An iron club having loft of 41-44 degrees, lie of 62-63 degrees and length of 35 1/2 inches. Giving distances of 80-150 yards for man and 65-135 yards for the ladies. Also called a **PITCHING NIBLICK**.

EGG:
> Referring to a ball on the putting green.

ELECTRIC CART:
> A motorized golf cart.

ELEVATED GREEN:
> A putting surface that is situated above the fairway usually on a hill.

ELECTRIC CART

ELEVATION FACTOR:
Holes that are uphill from tee to green play longer than those that are downhill from tee to green.

ELEPHANT'S REAR:
A poorly hit high shot that is "high and stinky".

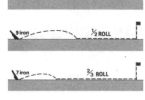

ELIGIBLE TOURNAMENT SCORE:
A tournament score made either within the last 12 matches or within the player's current 20 match score history.

EMBEDDED BALL:
A portion of the ball is buried below the ground.

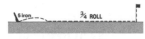

ENOUGH CLUB

ENGLISH:
Backspin applied to the ball. Also called **BACKSPIN** and **BITE**.

ENGLISH BET:
This golf game is played in threesomes. Six points are awarded on each hole. The player with the most points wins. Also called **SIX POINTS.**

ENOUGH CLUB:
The appropriate club for a given yardage.

EMBEDDED BALL

EQUIPMENT:
Anything that is used by a player or is carried or worn. Their ball in play is not included.

EQUITABLE STROKE CONTROL METHOD (ESC):
A method that specifies the maximum number you can receive on a hole based on your Course Handicap.

EQUITY:
A method of resolving disputes not covered by the rules.

ETIQUETTE:
A code of good manners and respect for other people on the golf course. It is common courtesy for your fellow golfers. A code of conduct.

EXACT HANDICAP:
An allowance of strokes that is deducted from a golfer's score for amateur golfers only. An Exact Handicap is computed and expressed to one decimal place.

EXECUTIVE COURSE:
Shorter in distance to allow for fast play, but longer than a pitch and putt.

EXPLODE:
To escape from a sand bunker with a shot that displaces a large amount of sand along with the ball. Also called **BLAST** and **EXPLOSION**.

EXPLOSION:
A shot hit from a sand trap carrying a large quantity of sand along with it. Also called a **BLAST** and **EXPLODE**.

EXPLOSION SHOT:
A golf recovery shot taken out of the sand trap displacing a lot of sand.

EXPLOSION

EXTENDED PLAY:
When play continues at a later time, usually the result of bad weather.

EXTENSION:
1. Achieving the desired length of the left arm at impact and the right arm at post impact in the swing. This position can be produced naturally by centrifugal force or by willfully applying leverage.
2. The position of the arms at the top of the backswing.

EXTRA HOLES:
Used when there is a tie between golfers after the competition has been completed. Extra holes will then be played to decide the winner.

FACE:
1. That part of the club head which comes into direct contact with the ball. The hitting part of the clubhead. Also called **CLUBFACE.**
2. An exposed bank of sand or steeply sloping sides of a bunker.
3. To courageously meet a change or confront difficulty.

FACE INSERT:
The extra hard impact area set into the face of a wooden club.

FACE PROGRESSION:
Measurement of the distance from the centerline of the shaft or hosel to the front leading portion of the clubface in both the irons and the woods.

FADE:
The flight of the ball that gradually curves from left to right. Also called **HEAVY.**

FADE SHOT:
The opposite of the draw. It is a controlled shot in which the ball starts to go to the left then turns back to the right into its intended line of flight.

FADE SPIN:
The rotation of the ball that causes it to fly left to right.

FADE

FADE

FAIR GREEN:
An obsolete term meaning the area of a links where the grass is relatively short and free of bushes and hazards. Also called the **FAIRWAY.**

FAIRWAY:
The short grassy area between the tee and the green. Also called **FAIR GREEN.**

FAIRWAY HIT:
Landing and stopping the ball on the fairway from the tee on holes greater than par three.

FAIRWAY OBSTACLE FACTOR:
The width of the landing area, which can be reduced by a dogleg, trees or tilting ground.

FAIRWAY WOOD:
Any wooden club that is not the driver.

FALL CLASSIC:
The annual **PGA TOUR QUALIFYING TOURNA-MENT**. Also called **Q-SCHOOL** and **QUALIFYING SCHOOL**.

FAN:
To miss the shot completely. Also called **AIRBALL, AIRSHOT** and **WHIFF**.

FANNING THE FACE:
An exaggerated rolling of the clubface into an open position early in the takeaway.

FANNING
THE FACE

FAST GREENS- SLOW GREENS:
Fast greens run the ball quicker in relation to the stroke needed to roll the ball to the target. Slower greens run the ball slower in relation to the stroke needed to roll the ball to the target.

FAT:
1. Describing a shot in which the clubhead strikes the ground before the ball, taking a large divot, so the ball does not travel as far as intended.
2. Referring to the widest, safest, and easiest part of the putting green. To hit to the widest and safest area on the green. Referring to the largest expanse of a putting green, making the easiest target for an approach without striving to get close to the pin.

FAT SHOT:
To strike the ground before the ball and then hitting the ball.

FEATHER:
1. To hit a long shot with gentle left to right (fade) flight which brings the ball down very lightly and without much roll.
2. To hit a controlled shot with a full swing.

FEATHERIE (FEATHERY):
An old leather ball stuffed with compressed goose and chicken feathers. Replaced by the gutta percha after 1848.

FEATHERY

FEEL:
The touch or good judgment in distance developed through practice. Also called **TOUCH**.

FEET:
Your feet are the base of your swing and must be firmly anchored.

FELLOW COMPETITOR:
The relationship between players in stroke play.

FESCUE:
A cool weather grass used for the rough on golf courses. Commonly found near salt water.

FIBER:
Insert material used in the faces of persimmon wood heads. Made of compressed and vulcanized paper. It is softer than most insert material and was preferred by the better golfer.

FIELD:
The players in a tournament.

FIGHT:
1. To struggle with a particular golfing problem. Example; the golfer who always hooks the ball is fighting the hook.
2. A struggle to stay in first place or in the running for first place.

FIND:
To arrive in a hazard or some other undesirable situation. Also called **FINDS**.

FINESSE:
To deliberately play other than a standard shot, in overcoming obstacles, weather, ground conditions, and the like.

FIRING PIN:
A circular piece of metal, usually brass or aluminum, installed in the center of some types of inserts.

FIRST CUT:
Strip of rough at the edge of the fairway.

FIRST OFF:
Golfers beginning their round before everyone else.

FIND

FIRST TEE FEARS:
Fear of hitting off the first tee. Also called **FIRST TEE JITTERS** and **FIRST TEE SYNDROME**.

FIVE-IRON:
An iron club having loft of 29-32 degrees, lie of 59-61 degrees, and length of 37 inches. Giving distance of 169-190 yards for the men and 135-165 yards for the ladies. Also called the **MASHIE**.

FIVE-WOOD:
A wood club having loft of 21-23 degrees, lie of 55-56 degrees, and length of 41 inches. Giving distance of 180-210 yards for the men and 155-175 yards for the ladies. Also called the **BAFFLE**.

FLAG:
1. A piece of cloth attached to the top of the flagstick.
2. The marker that shows the position of the hole on the green. Also called **FLAGSTICK** and **PIN**.

FLAGGING IT:
Hitting the flagstick with the ball.

FLAGSTICK:
Placed in the center of the cup on the green to indicate the location of the hole. Also called **FLAG** and **PIN**.

FIVE-IRON

FLAG EVENTS:
1. A player carries their flag until their net score has fallen behind the course using the hole stroke indexes.
2. Games in which the best is marked by a flag on the course green, fairway, etc. Some examples would be: closest to the pin, longest drive, and longest putt.

FLAG TOURNAMENT:
Using full handicaps, the golfers continue playing until they use up the number of strokes in their handicaps. The player who plays the most holes wins.

FLAME BROILED:
A drive that is hit hard and long. Also called a **WHOPPER** and **BOMB**.

FLANGE:
1. A projecting piece of clubhead behind the sole.
2. The trailing edge of an iron or putter.

FLANGE PUTTER:
A type of putter.

FLANGE PUTTER

FLASH TRAP:
A shallow or small bunker.

FLAT BELLIES:
The young and thin golfers on the **PGA TOUR**.

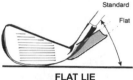

FLAT LIE

FLAT LIE:
1. The lie angle of a clubhead and the ball which is flatter than the norm.
2. A club having a relatively wide angle between the head and the shaft; the lie of a club relatively wide-angled.

FLAT STICK:
Another name for the **PUTTER**.

FLAT SWING:
A swing that is less upright than normal. This is an improper swing. A swing moving in a relatively horizontal plane. Sometimes occurs when the clubhead is carried back in a flat manner on the in to out swing path.

FLAT SWING

FLEX:
1. The amount of bend or the degree of stiffness of the club shaft.
2. The amount of bend in the knees at address.

FLEX POINT:
That part of a club's shaft which bends the most. The Flex Point is the point or region of the club shaft which can bend (flex) the most. Lower flex points tend to create higher ball trajectories. Also called the **KICK POINT**.

FLIER:
1. A ball that flies a greater distance than normal.
2. A shot struck from long grass that flies much farther than normal because of a lack of backspin.

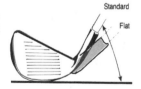

FLIER LIE

FLIER LIE:
A good lie in the rough.

FLIER SHOT:
A ball hit from wet grass, caught between the clubface and the ball. The ball gets no grip on the clubface and the grass acts as grease.

FLIP SHOT:
A short, delicately hit approach shot of high trajectory played with a highly lofted iron.

FLIP WEDGE:
A short, less-than-full wedge shot usually played to the green. Similar to a **HALF WEDGE**.

FLIGHT:
1. The flight is the path the ball takes as it travels through the air. The flight of the ball is determined by the loft of the club, stance, hands and swing path.
2. In tournament play, the division of players with players of equal ability being placed in the same flight. Sixteen is usually the number of players in a flight. However, any number of players may be in a flight.

FLIGHT

FLOATER:
1. A ball which soars high and lightly in the air.
2. A ball struck from deep grass which comes out slowly and travels shorter than normal due to a heavy cushioning of the blow from excess grass between the ball and clubface. Opposite of a flier.
3. A golf ball that will float in water.

FLOP SHOT:
A loose-wristed pitch in which the club is taken abruptly up on the backswing then dropped lazily and steeply down, sliding the clubhead underneath the ball.

FLORIDA SCRAMBLE:
This golf game is similar to the normal scramble, except the player whose shot was selected must sit out on the next shot.

FLUB:
To hit the ball weakly and only roll a few feet or a near miss.

FLUFF:
To mis-hit a shot.

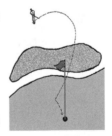

FLOP SHOT

FLUFFY (FLUFF):
A ball that is sitting up in the grass. Also called a **FLUFFY LIE**.

FLY:
1. To hit a shot that completely carries over the intended target.
2. The distance of the ball in the air.
3. A ball landing from the air without having bounced. Also referred to as hitting on the fly.

FLYING ELBOW:
The outward movement of the right elbow. This is a faulty movement and causes a mis-hit shot.

FLY THE GREEN:
A shot hit beyond the green.

FOCUS:
The central point of attraction and attention. To concentrate and direct your attention on a golf shot.

FOG:
Scottish term meaning growth of moss or long grass.

FOLLOW-THROUGH:
It is the continuation of the swing after the ball has been hit.

FOLLOW THROUGH

FOOTWORK:
It is the positioning of the feet at address and how they react during the swing.

FOOZLED:
Badly miss hit shot.

FORE:
It is the warning shout to alert other golfers that a hit ball is in their direction.

FORECADDIE:
An extra caddie posted at driving or long iron distance to mark the ball after it has stopped.

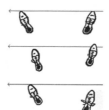

FOREWEIGHTING:
Depositing weight in the face area of the club, done to bring the center of gravity forward in the clubhead. Promoting a lower shot trajectory.

FOOTWORK

FORGED:
A method of making a golf club. The club is formed by a mechanical or hydraulic press. The process may or may not include heating of the metal.

FORGING:
1. Working a piece of metal into a desired shape by pressing or hammering.
2. One of the processes for forming iron heads.

FORGED IRONS:
Clubs made one by one, without molds.

FORM:
A golfer's standard of play based on performance.

FORWARD PRESS:
A preliminary movement before the backswing starts.

FORWARD PRESS

FORWARD SWING:
Once the backswing has been completed, the motion of the body, arms, hands and club in the opposite direction through the ball. Also called the **DOWNSWING**.

FOUR JACK:
To take four putts on the putting surface green. Also called **FOUR PUTT**.

FOURS:
A score averaging four strokes for each hole.

FOURSOME:
1. A golf game that is played by two players a side, but both players use the same ball and take turns hitting.
2. When a group of four golfers play a round.

FOUR-IRON

FOUR BALL:
Is a match involving four players in which two play their better ball against the better ball of two other players. It can be either stroke or match play.

FOUR-IRON:
An iron club having loft of 25-28 degrees, lie of 58-60 degrees, and length of 37 1/2 inches. Giving distance of 155-200 yards for the men and 145-175 yards for the ladies. Also called the **MASHIE-IRON** and **SAMMY**.

FOUR-PUTT:
To take four putts on the putting green. Also called **FOUR JACK**.

FOUR-WOOD:
A wood club having loft of 18-20 degrees, lie of 55-57 degrees, and length of 411/2 inches. Giving distance of 190-220 yards for the men and 165-185 yards for the ladies. Also called the **CLEEK** or **WOODEN SPOON**.

FOUR-WOOD

FREAK:
   1. Opposed to the traditions or the rules of golf, or both.
   2. Something odd happening on the course.

FREE DROP:
   A drop where no penalty stroke is incurred.

FREQUENCY MATCHING:
   Method of measuring consistency of shaft flex throughout a set of clubs. Also called **FREQUENCY**.

FRINGE:
   The grass immediately surrounding the green. Also called the **APRON, COLLAR** and **FROGHAIR**.

FRIED EGG:
   A ball half buried in the sand.

FROG HAIR:
   Short grass bordering the edge of the green. Also called the **FRINGE** and **APRON**.

FRIED EGG

FRONT NINE:
   The first nine holes of the round. Also called **FIRST NINE, OUT, FRONT SIDE** and **OUTWARD NINE**.

FROSTY:
   To score an eight on any given hole. Also called a **SNOWMAN**.

FULL SET:
   There are 16 basic clubs in a full set. The rules allow the golfer to carry 14 clubs for playing a round.

FULL SWING:
   The longest possible swing you can take.

FULL SET

FUNDAMENTALS:
   1. The essential parts of a good swing.
   2. The Forming of a foundation or basis for any given golf shot or swing.

FUZZY:
   A green that has not been mowed and the grass is longer than what it should be. The ball rolls much slower.

GALLERY:
Spectators at a tournament.

GALLERYITE:
A spectator at a match or tournament.

GAMBLING:
1. Taking a risky shot.
2. Placing a bet.
3. The USGA does not object to gambling since the wagering is done between the golfers and not any outside source.

GAP WEDGE:
A modern wedge which loft fits between a PW and SW, usually 52 degrees on the club face.

GARBAGE:
This golf game can be played with any number of players. Points are awarded to the player who can achieve good results in different shot situations. Also called **TRASH**. The usual point system is as follows;

HOLE IN ONE	100 Points
DOUBLE EAGLE	100 Points
EAGLE	50 Points
BIRDIE	10 Points
GREENIES	1 Point
ARNIES	1 Point
TIGER	1 Point
SANDIES	1 Point
BARKIES	1 Point
HOGAN	1 Point
WATSON/CRENSHAW	1 Point
GURGLIE/WHALIE	1 Point
POLIE	1 Point
CHI-CHI	1 Point
SNAKIE	MINUS 1 POINT
DOUBLE SNAKIE	MINUS 1 POINT

GAS:
Referring to the ball's momentum. A putt that stops before falling into the cup is said to have "run out of gas".

GATEWAY:
The part of a fairway that leads to the green, especially if flanked by hills or hazards.

GATEWAY

GENTLEMEN GAME:
Expression used to describe the dignity and respect for the game of golf. Also called the **LADIES GAME**.

GEOMETRY:
A term used to describe the diameter and contours of graphite shafts.

GET DOWN:
1. A term used to describe the act of putting the ball into the hole.
2. Sinking the putt and ending the hole. For example, "He needs to get down in three."
3. Expression used by the golfer when a ball is hit too far or off line.
4. Feeling depressed about your golf game or score.

GET LEGS:
An expression used to "encourage" the ball to continue rolling when it appears that the ball will stop short of the hole. The term is usually used with a chip shot or putt.

GET UP:
1. Expression used to urge a putt or shot to travel closer to the hole.
2. Getting yourself into a positive mental attitude before taking the shot.

GHIN:
Golf Handicap Information Network.

GIMMICK

GIMMICK:
Any idea, device, scheme or stunt used to replace the fundamentals of golf. Most gimmicks are tricky and will hurt your golf game. However, some gimmicks may improve your game.

GIMMIE:
When a ball is so close to the hole it is virtually impossible to miss it and it is given by the opposing player or team. It is counted as one stroke. Also known as **DEAD, GIVE** and **KICK IN**.

GINSBURG:
The option on the tee to hit a second shot. Also called a **MULLIGAN** and **BREAKFAST BALL**.

GINTY:
A specialty club used for hitting out of troubled lies or hazards.

GIVE:
When a ball is so close to the hole it is virtually impossible to miss it and it is given by the opposing player or team. It is counted as one stroke. Also known as **DEAD, GIMMIE** and **KICK IN**.

GLOBE:
To miss the ball. An obsolete term meaning to make a stroke that fails to hit the ball.

GO TO SCHOOL:
To watch the path of a previous putt over a certain area of the green as a method for determining the roll of that green. Also called **GOING TO SCHOOL.**

GO TO THE HILL:
To move to the practice area, usually after an unsatisfactory round.

GO TO THE WINDOW:
To collect money in a professional tournament.

GOAT FARM:
A poorly maintained golf course.

GOBBLE

GOBBLE:
An obsolete slang term meaning a hard hit putt that holes.

GOLF:
A game that is played on an outdoor course, requiring the participant to propel a small ball from one designated point to another in the fewest possible strokes, by means of a specially designed club, and sinking the ball into a hole 4 1/2 inches in size on a manicured putting surface.

GOLFDOM:
The world of golf.

GOLFER:
A player of golf.

GOLFIANA:
Matters, literature, or artifacts belonging to golf.

GOLFIC:
A Scottish term refering to anything relating to golf.

GOLFING:
The playing of golf or relating to golf.

GOLF BALL

GOLF ASSOCIATION:
An organization of golf clubs formed in order to conduct competitions for amateur and professional golfers to promote and conserve the best interest and spirit of golf within a region.

GOLF BALL:
The spherical object used in playing golf. Also called **BALL.**

GOLF CLUB:

1. A "golf club" in official golfing language is an organization of at least ten individual members operating under bylaw and having committees whose responsibility it is to supervise golf activities and maintain the integrity of the USGA Handicap System. The USGA requires that club members have a reasonable opportunity to play golf on a regular basis and to return their scorecards or scores for posting. An organization of amateur golfers at a public golf course may be considered a golf club if it meets all other requirements for a club.
2. Any of the various tools used in golf to strike the ball, consisting essentially of a thin shaft with a grip for holding it and a clubhead of wood or iron.

GOLF GLOVE:

Usually worn to maintain grip with the club. Generally worn on the left hand of the right handed golfer. Worn on the right hand of the left handed golfer.

GOLF GLOVE

GOLF RANGE:

A facility where a golfer may hit balls to improve his swing. They sometimes includes a short-game practice area. Also called a **PRACTICE CENTER** and **RANGE**.

GOLF WIDOW (ER):

The slang term for the non-golfing spouse of a golfer.

GOOSENECK PUTTER:

Having the neck of a club curved so that the heel is slightly offset from the line of the shaft.

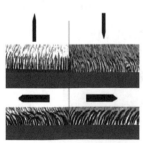

GOOSE NECK

GORILLA:

One who drives the ball for a long distance off the tee. Also called a **MONSTER DRIVER**.

GORSE BUSH:

A shrub primarily found on link land type courses. It is a spiny evergreen with bright yellow flowers. Also called **WHIN**.

GRAIN:

The way the grass is growing or is cut.

GRAINY:

Having strong grain.

GRAND SLAM:

Refers to the four major championships:
1. The Masters
2. The U.S. Open
3. The British Open
4. The PGA Championship

GRAIN

GRAPHITE:
Light weight material used to make golf clubs. A pure carbon mineral made into fibers, mixed with resin, and formed into a golf shaft.

GRASS BUNKER:
Like a sand trap but instead of sand, grass is used.

GRASS CLUB:
Obsolete term referring to a driver with slightly more loft than the straight-faced driver or play club. Also called **GRASSED** or **GRASSED DRIVER**.

GRASSCUTTER:
A hard hit ball, traveling low and skimming the grass.

GRASSED:
Obsolete term meaning a wooden lofted club-face.

GREEN

GREEN:
1. The specially prepared putting surface. Also known as the **DANCE FLOOR, PUTTING GREEN** and **PUTTING SURFACE**.
2. Chiefly Scottish term meaning a golf course.

GREENIES:
A bet won by the player whose first shot finishes closest to the hole on a par 3. Variation, if the player three putts he loses the greenie. The greenie then goes to the second closest to the hole.

GREENSKEEPER:
The employee of the club who is responsible for the maintenance of the course.

GREENKEEPING:
The science and profession of maintaining and managing a golf course.

GREENS IN REGULATION:
From the tee box, an average golfer should reach the green in a specified number of strokes. This number is determined by the par value of the hole:
Par 3 hole: 1 stroke
Par 4 hole: 2 strokes
Par 5 hole: 3 strokes
Par 6 hole: 4 strokes
This is considered reaching the green in regulation. Also called **GIR**.

GREENSIDE

GREENSIDE:
A ball that lies adjacent to the putting green.

GREENSOME:
Informal format which calls for both players forming a partnership to drive and then select the better placed ball to continue playing the hole by hitting alternating shots played in foursomes.

GREEN COMMITTEE:
Members of a golf club who are responsible for the maintenance and management of the course.

GREEN FEE:
The amount of money charged by the golf course to play a round of golf. Also called **GREENS FEE**.

GREEN JACKET:
A prize awarded to the winner of The Masters Tournament.

GREEN PROPAGANDA SWEEP:
Any erroneous golf instruction deliberately intended to confuse or impair an individual golfer. Misrepresentation of golf instruction. To move on out in the misrepresentation of golf.

GREEN TARGET:
The size, shape, slope, firmness and the length of the approach to the green.

GREMLIN:
Negative thoughts about golf or your shot making ability.

GRINDER:
A serious player who is all business on the golf course.

GRIP:
1. The way the player holds the club.
2. A piece of leather or rubber on the handle of the shaft.

GRIP IT AND RIP IT:
To walk up to the ball and just take a healthy swing at it with no **SWINGING THOUGHTS**.

GROCERY MONEY:
1. Money won on the tour.
2. Money won on a bet.

GRIP

GROOVE:
1. The consistent path or sequence of movements followed by the swing of a consistently accurate player. To habituate the swing or a stroke into a consistent and accurate pattern by practice. The path a club takes in a consistent, repetitious swing.
2. The parallel lines on a clubface designed to keep the ball from running up the face. Linear scoring on the face of the club.

GROOVED:
Habituated by practice into a consistent and accurate pattern.

GROSS SCORE:
Your gross score is the number of strokes you take to complete a hole or a round before you deduct your handicap.

GROUNDER:
A golf shot that frequents the ground. Also called a **WORM BURNER**.

GROUNDING THE CLUB:
When the clubhead is placed on the ground behind the ball. Also called **SOLING THE CLUB**.

GROUNDING
THE CLUB

GROUND UNDER REPAIR:
The area of the golf course closed off for repair. Any ball landing in it must be removed, without penalty.

GROUP LESSON:
An instructional session which includes five or more pupils with one or more instructors.

GROW TEETH:
Expression used when the golfer wants the ball to stop rolling after the ball has landed on the green. Also called **BITE, CHEW** and **BITE YOU BALL**.

GUARDED GREEN:
A green surrounded with hazards and other difficulties making the approach to it difficult.

GURGLIE:
A player who has hit the water hazard and still makes par or better in regulation. Also called a **FISH, FISHIE** or **WHALIE**.

GUTTIE or GITTY:
Refers to the **GUTTA PERCHA** ball type.

GUTTA PERCHA

GUTTA PERCHA:
Material used in the manufacture of early golf balls. It was a hard, molded substance made from the sap of several types of Malaysian trees. These balls were in use from 1848 until the early 1900.

GUTTY-PERKY:
Scottish. Variant of **GUTTA PERCHA**.

HACK:
1. To chop down violently at the ball.
2. To make bad shots.
3. To play bad golf.

HACKER:
A poor player. Also called a **DUFFER** and **DUBBER**.

HALF:
1. A match or hole is halved if both players' or teams' scores are the same at the end of the match or hole and both are credited with a tie and neither side wins the hole. Also called **HALVE**.
2. An expression used to indicate a handicap allowance, meaning a stroke on every other hole.

HALF SET:
Either the odd or even irons, two woods and a putter. A half set of clubs is all a beginning golfer needs to start playing.

HALF SHOT:
A shot played with less than the normal length back-swing and effort, designed to achieve around 50 percent of the regular distance for the club. Also called **HALF SWING**.

HALF SHOT

HALVE:
A match or hole is halved if both players' or teams' scores are the same at the end of the match or hole and both are credited with a tie and neither side wins the hole. Also called **HALF**.

HALVED:
A term used when players have the same score on a hole in match play.

HALVE A HOLE:
In match play, refers to a draw when both opponents take the same number of shots to complete the hole.

HALVE A MATCH:
In match play, refers to a draw when both opponents have won the same number of holes in the round.

HAM AND EGGS:
When you and your partner play well on alternating holes, making good teamwork.

HAND MASHIE:
The five finger swipe at the ball to improve the position of the lie.

HANDICAP:
1. The number of strokes a player deducts from his actual score to meet his opponent on equal terms. The number of artificial strokes a player receives to adjust his scoring ability to the common level of scratch or zero-handicap golf. The handicap system allows all golfers to compete fairly on any course.
2. Handicap is also the grade given to a hole as indicated on the score card. The most difficult hole on the course is stroke 1 while the easiest is stroke 18.

HANDICAP ACQUISITION:
You must play at a golf course that belongs to the USGA, a state or local association. A small fee is paid and you are placed on the list or computer. Then you must play 10 to 20 rounds before your handicap is established. The **HANDICAP SYSTEM** uses the best 10 scores out of your last 20 scores to calculate an accurate handicap.

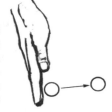

HAND MASHIE

HANDICAP ALLOWANCE:
The handicap allowance is that part of a handicap that can be used in a given form of play. Allowances vary for different forms of play and are designed to produce equalized competition.

HANDICAP COMMITTEE:
The committee of a golf club that ensures compliance with the **USGA HANDICAP SYSTEM**. Any club using the **USGA HANDICAP SYSTEM** is required to have a handicap committee.

HANDICAP DIFFERENTIAL:
1. A Handicap Differential helps to determine a player's handicap index. To compute this, subtract the **USGA COURSE RATING** from the **ADJUSTED GROSS SCORE**. Multiply the difference by 113 and finally divide the resulting number by the **USGA SLOPE RATING**.
2. The difference between a player's adjusted gross score and the **USGA COURSE RATING** of the golf course on which the score was just made.

HANDICAP FACTOR:
The handicap factor is determined by subtracting the course rating for the golf course where the round was played from the golfer's gross score.

HANDICAP INDEX:
Used to indicate a measurement of a player's potential scoring ability on a course of standard playing difficulty. It is expressed as a number and used for conversion to a course handicap.

HANDICAP PLAYER:

A handicap player is one whose score for an average round of golf is higher than par golf and, as a result, is given a handicap.

HANDICAP SHEET:

A computer printout with a golfer's handicap listed for the month accompanied by the breakdown of his scores.

HANDICAP STROKE HOLE:

A stroke hole is one on which a golfer applies a handicap stroke. The order in which handicap strokes are designated appears on the scorecard. The toughest hole on a course is called the number one stroke hole. The easiest hole is the number 18 stroke hole. Also called **HOLE HANDICAP.**

HANDICAP STROKE PLAY:

A golf game in which players play 18 holes of stroke play golf. Full handicaps are used.

HARDPAN

HANDICAP SYSTEM:

A system designed to give golfers an opportunity to compete on equal terms against better golfers.

HANGING LIE:

When your ball is resting on a downhill slope. Also called **HANGING**.

HAPPY FEET:

A nervous condition, when the golfer cannot keep his or her feet still while taking the shot. Also called **JELLY LEGS**.

HARDPAN:

Very firm turf or very hard ground. Hard ground usually without grass.

HASKELL:

Forerunner to the modern golf ball. Introduced in the early 1900's to replace the **GUTTY**. Named after Coburn Haskell, an American who invented the machine to wind rubber thread under tension around a central core.

HAWK:

A golf game played in threesomes. The player with the most points wins.

HASKELL

HAZARD:

Any permanent obstacle on a golf course. A natural or man-made obstacle that interferes with play. According to the Rules of Golf, a hazard not only includes bunkers and water hazards, but also other objects such as roads, walls, trees, and bushes which present playing hazards when encountered on the golf course.

HCP:
An abbreviation for Playing Handicap.

HEAD:
The head is the part of the golf club used to hit the ball. It is made up of several parts: the sole, heel, toe, neck, and face.

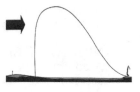

HEADWIND

HEADWIND:
The wind coming into the golfer. As you are looking at the target, the wind is blowing and hitting your face. Also called **UPWIND**.

HEAD WIDTH:
The distance from the farthest forward point of the leading edge to the farthest rear point of the back line.

HEEL:
1. The heel is the portion of the clubhead located nearest the shaft.
2. The term is also used to describe a ball hit from this part of the club which travels at a right angle to the line of play.

HEEL AND TOE WEIGHTING:
Club method of construction that distributes weight around the perimeter of the clubhead. Designed to improve off-center hits by adding weight away from the sweet spot.

HEELED SHOT:
A shot that is hit off the heel of the club. One in which the ball is struck on that portion of the clubface between the hosel and the center of the face.

HEELED SHOT

HI - LOW TOURNAMENT:
Golf game in tournament format, based on the better ball score of each team, using full handicap.

HICKORY:
Hardwood from the native American tree used between 1900 and the 1920's to make golf shafts.

HIGH - LOW:
The pairing of two players in a tournament, one with a high handicap and the other with a low handicap.

HIGH HANDICAPPER:
A golfer who receives a high number of handicap strokes, 30 or more, usually a beginner.

HIGH SIDE:
The area above the hole on a sloping green.

HIT:
To play a shot or stroke. Also called **SHOOT**.

HITTER:
A player using a style of striking the ball which employs considerable thrust or leverage to power the club.

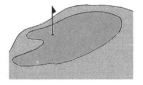

HIGH SIDE

HIT A BRICK:
1. An expression used to encourage the ball to stop from rolling past the hole.
2. A term used when a player chips or putts the ball well past the target.

HIT A HOUSE:
1. An expression used to encourage the ball to stop from rolling past the hole.
2. A term used when a player chips or putts the ball well past the target.

HIT IT SIDEWAYS:
Expression used when you did not play well. Something you would say after a bad round of golf.

HITTING AREA:
Part of the swing from where the club is parallel to the ground on the downswing to just after impact.

HITTING EARLY:
Starting to uncock the wrists too soon in the downswing.

HITTING AREA

HITTING LATE:
Delaying the uncocking of the wrists in an attempt to increase clubhead acceleration and therefore hit the ball a greater distance.

HOG'S BACK:
A ridge of ground or a hole having a ridge on a fairway.

HOGAN:
When a player's shot lands on the fairway and hits the green in regulation and makes par or better. This is named after the great Ben Hogan who used to do it most the time.

HOGANS:
A golf game played on par four and par five holes. When a golfer hits the fairway, then hit the green in regulation and makes par or better. The game does not include par three holes.

HOLD:
When the ball hits the ground and stays in one place with little roll or bounce.

HOLE:
1. A target for the ball. Each hole measures 4-1/4 inches (12cm) in diameter. A piece of earth cut out of the ground on finely manicured grass into which a little white ball is hit. Marked with a flagstick. Also called **CUP**.
2. The act of putting the ball into the cup.

HOLABLE:
A putt within reasonable distance for holing out. A makeable putt.

HOLED:
A ball has been "holed" when it is completely below the lip of the hole and is at rest within it.

HOLER:
A successful putter or putt.

HOLED

HOLE HANDICAP:
Each scorecard indicates a handicap number for each hole. The lower the number, the harder the hole is to play. Some courses split odd and even handicap numbers between the front nine and back nine while others handicap all eighteen holes together. Also **HANDICAP STROKE HOLE**.

HOLE HIGH:
A ball that comes to rest, on either right or left of the flag, but level with the hole on the green or to the sides of it. Also called **PIN HIGH**.

HOLE IN ONE:
To play a hole in one stroke. Also called an **ACE**.

HOLE INDICATOR

HOLE INDICATOR:
The second flag on the flagstick. Positioned below the top flag to indicate the location of the hole in relation to the green. When the second flag is high on the flagstick, the hole is placed in the back of the green. When the second flag is placed in the middle of the flagstick, the hole is in the middle of the green and when the second flag is placed low on the flagstick, the hole is in the front of the green. Also called **INTERMEDIATE FLAG**.

HOLE MAKE-UP:
Elements or distinguishing features of a hole. Also called **MAKE-UP OF A HOLE** and **COURSE DESIGN**.

HOLE OUT:
To play a shot into the hole.

HOLLYWOOD:
1. To look and act successful.
2. What you are when everything is going right.

HOLLYWOOD HANDICAP:
A slang expression for a handicap which is too low, making the golfer sound like a star.

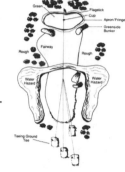

HOLE MAKE-UP

HOME:
Refers to the green. Also called the **PUTTING SURFACE, PUTTING GREEN** and **DANCE FLOOR**.

HOMEWARD NINE:
The back nine holes on the golf course. Also called **BACK NINE, SECOND NINE, BACK HALF, LAST NINE, IN NINE, BACK SIDE, BACK, IN, SECOND HALF, HOMEWARD NINE, LAST HALF** or **INWARD HALF**.

HOME COURSE:
The golf course where you received your handicap.

HOME GREEN:
The putting green on the eighteenth hole.

HOME HOLE:
1. The eighteenth hole or the final hole played.
2. The nineteenth hole or clubhouse.

HOME OF GOLF

HOME MATCH:
A match made up of rounds played on the home course of each participant or group.

HOME OF GOLF:
Traditional reference to St. Andrews, in Scotland.

HOME PRO:
A professional who maintains his position at a golf club to teach and play only in local events.

HONOURABLE COMPANY OF EDINBURGH GOLFERS
The distinction of being recognized as the oldest golf club in the world falls to the Honourable Company of Edinburgh Golfers, now based at Muirfeld on the Firth of Forth to the east of Edinburgh. It was however located at Leith in 1744, just outside the Scottish capital of Edinburgh. The club has maintained continuous records since its inception, although the scene of its activities was moved from Leith in 1831 to Musselburgh in 1836 and eventually to Muirfeld in 1891. In 1744, to mark the creation of the club, Edinburgh Town Council presented the Honourable Company with a silver club to be contested by the members. Thus the first club competition was born. John Rattray was the winner and hence became its first captain.

HONOR:
The privilege of playing first off the tee. Usually the person who wins the previous hole or round shoots first.

HOODED CLUB

HOOD:
Shutting the face of the club and playing the ball closer to the right foot than normal. Also called **SHUT POSITION**.

HOODED CLUB:
Tilting the toe end of the club towards the hole. It lessens the loft of the club. Also called **CLOSED FACE POSITION**.

HOODING:
De-lofting the club by advancing the grip forward toward the target or reducing loft during the swing, but keeping the face square to the target line. It does not mean closing the face, as it is so often misconstrued, although when closing the face, the club may be hooded as well.

HOOK:
The flight of a golf ball that curves severely to the left.

HOOKER:
A golfer who consistently hits the ball to the left.

HOOKING SPIN:
It is the rotation put on the ball that spins the ball from the inside out, causing the ball to fly to the left.

HOOK

HOOK SHOT:
A shot that bends sharply to the left of the target for the right-hand golfer.

HORIZONTAL:
The desired position at the top of the backswing, with the clubshaft parallel to the ground. Also called **PARALLEL**.

HORIZONTAL AXIS (BALL):

An imaginary line running through the center of the ball in a horizontal plane. Striking the ball with the clubface below this point causes it to be airborne. Striking above it will cause the ball to be topped.

HORSESHOE:

When the ball goes around the edge of the cup and comes back toward you.

HORIZONTAL AXIS

HOSEL:

The hosel is a fixture between the clubhead and club shaft. Some say the type and size of hosel can affect the weight distribution of the clubhead and possibly the feel. Generally, it most often affects the off-set of the clubhead.

HOT:

1. A ball traveling at a fast rate of speed without backspin, and hitting the ground, and rolling for a good distance.
2. When a ball is about to bc lifted, touched, or hit by the wrong player.
3. Anytime a golfer is playing extremely well. Also called **ZONE**.

HOVERING CLUB:

1. The position of the clubhead as it sweeps the ball off the tee.
2. Used instead of soling the club on the ground; the club is kept slightly off the turf at address.

HUMPING IT:

When a caddie or golfer carries the golf bag on his or her shoulder instead of using a cart.

HUNCHER:

The player who illegally moves the ball closer to the hole.

HOVERING CLUB

HUNCHING:

1. Replacing a marked ball closer to the hole then originally marked.
2. Leaning too far over the ball at address.
3. A vague feeling or suspicion.

HUNG IT OUT:

A golfer attempting to play a draw, but hits a straight shot instead. Also called **HANGING IT OUT**.

HUSTLER:

A golfer who plays for a living and plays better than what he claims.

IDENTIFYING BALL:

Except in hazards, a golfer may, without penalty, lift their ball and clean it for purposes of identification, then the ball is replaced in the exact location from which it was lifted.

IFFY LIE:

A lie where it is uncertain how the ball will react when struck.

IMBEDDED BALL:

Ball that imbeds itself in wet or muddy turf. Same as the **EMBEDDED BALL**.

IMPACT:

The moment the clubhead contacts the ball.

IMBEDDED BALL

IMPACT BOARD:

A board designed to fit a golfer to clubs with the correct lie. Balls are hit off the board, leaving impact marks on the sole of the club, indicating how far from center the lie of the club is.

IMPEDIMENT:

Loose debris that can be moved from around the ball as long as the ball does not move.

IMPOSSIBLE LIE:

A ball that cannot be hit from the position in which it rests.

IMPROVE YOUR LIE:

This is cheating. To move the ball to make the shot easier.

IN AND OUT

IN AND OUT:

The swing path on which the clubhead travels from the inside of the ball-to-target line to outside the ball-to-target line. On this occasion, the ball will start right of the target. Also called **INSIDE-TO-OUT** and **IN-TO-OUT**.

IN MY POCKET:
Expression used to tell the other members of your group that you have picked up your ball and have conceded the hole. Also called **IN THE LINEN**.

IN THE BAG:
1. Expression used when a golfer is confident in his or her ability to pull off a certain shot. Also called **BAGFUL**.
2. When a golfer is in a situation where it is unquestionable about him or her winning the round or tournament.

IN THE HUNT:
1. When a player is looking for his or her lost ball.
2. Expression used when any player has a chance of winning a tournament heading into the final round. Also called **IN THE RUNNING** and **IN THE GAME**.

IN THE LEATHER

IN THE LEATHER:
A term in friendly matches allowing a putt which lies no more than the length of the leather wrapping on the player's putter from the cup, or the distance of the putter head. Not legally permitted by the rules of golf.

IN THE LINEN:
Expression used to tell the other members of your group that you have picked up your ball and have conceded the hole. Also called **IN MY POCKET**.

IN THE RUNNING:
Expression used when any player has a chance of winning a tournament heading into the final round. Also called **IN THE HUNT** and **IN THE GAME**.

IN TO IN:
The swing pattern which produces a straight flying ball, provided the clubface is square and the ball is hit in the center of its equator. Also called **INSIDE-TO-IN**.

IN YOUR POCKET:
Term sometimes used when a player has picked up the ball before putting out, usually because the maximum number of strokes has been used or the last putt was given to another player.

IN:
The last nine holes of an eighteen-hole course. Also called **BACK NINE, SECOND NINE, LAST NINE, IN NINE, BACK SIDE, BACK HOLES, BACK, SECOND HALF, HOMEWARD NINE, LAST HALF** or **INWARD HALF**.

INACTIVE SEASON:
The time period, determined by an authorized golf association, during which golfers can not use scores for handicap purposes.

INCONSISTENT:
The player who is always changing his swing and does not play a consistent game of golf.

INDIVIDUAL HANDICAP:
The rating each golfer is given by a sanctioned golf association.

INLAND:
1. A course not situated by the sea; not being a seaside links land course of the traditionally classic Scottish kind.
2. Ball in play within the course limits and not out of bounds.

INPLAY:
A ball is in play the moment it is hit until the moment it is holed out. If it goes out of bounds or is lost, it is no longer in play.

INSERT:
A piece of material placed into the face of a wood head, designed to improve the durability of the clubface on impact. Usually made of Epoxy, Cycolac, Aluminum, Fiber or Graphite.

INSIDE:
Nearer the hole than one's opponent or one's opponent's ball.

INSIDE THE LINE:
The area on player's side of the intended line as he or she addresses the ball.

INSIDE-TO-IN

INSIDE TO IN:
The swing pattern which produces a straight flying ball, provided the clubface is square and the ball is hit in the center of its equator. Also called **IN-TO-IN**.

INSIDE-TO-OUT:
The swing path on which the clubhead travels from the inside of the ball-to-target line to out- side the ball-to-target line. Also called **IN-TO-OUT** and **IN AND OUT**.

INTENDED LINE:
The path on which you imagine the ball flying from your club to the target. Also called **INTENDED LINE OF FLIGHT**.

INTERLOCKING GRIP:
In an interlocking grip, the forefinger of the left hand locks with the pinky finger of the right hand for a right-handed golfer.

INTERLOCKING
GRIP

INTERMEDIATE FLAG:
The second flag on the flagstick. It is positioned below the top flag to indicate the location of the hole in relation to the green. When the second flag is high on the flagstick, the hole is placed in the back of the green. When the second flag is placed in the middle of the flagstick, the hole is in the middle of the green and when the second flag is placed low on the flagstick, the hole is in the front of the green. Also called **HOLE INDICATOR**.

INTERMEDIATE TARGET:
A leaf, rock, divot or other object or mark just in front of the ball and directly between ball and the target, used as an alignment aid.

INTERMEDIATE
TARGET

IN-TO-OUT:
The swing path on which the clubhead travels from the inside of the ball-to-target line to out side the ball-to-target line. On this occasion, the ball will start right of the target. Also called **INSIDE TO OUT** and **IN AND OUT**.

INVESTMENT CAST:
The process for making clubheads that entails pouring molten metal into wax molds. These molds are created or cast from an original steel die.

INWARD HALF:
The last nine holes of an eighteen-hole course. Also called **BACK NINE, SECOND NINE, LAST NINE, IN NINE, BACK SIDE, BACK HOLES, IN, SECOND HALF, HOMEWARD NINE, LAST HALF** or **BACK**.

IRON:
1. Metal headed clubs that are not wood, except for the putter.
2. A lofted club with a metal head. The loft on the face becomes larger as the number of the club increases.

IRON COVERS:
Equipment used to protect the head of the iron clubs.

IRON COVERS

IRON PLAY:
1. Taking a stroke with an iron club.
2. Playing a round with all iron clubs.

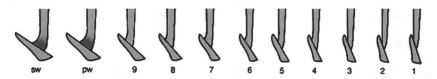

| sw | pw | 9 | 8 | 7 | 6 | 5 | 4 | 3 | 2 | 1 |

IRONS

IS THAT ANY GOOD:
Rhetorical question posed to confuse, irritate, and stun opponents.

JACK AND JILL EVENT:

A tournament played by one-man and one-woman teams.

JAIL:

When the ball lies in trouble that seems impossible to hit out of or escape from.

JAWS:

Expression used when a ball that is putted stops inches short of the cup.

JAIL

JELLY LEGS:

A nervous condition when the golfer cannot keep his or her feet still while taking the shot. Also called **HAPPY FEET**.

JERK:

1. To hit the ball from a bad lie, rough or sand with a downward cutting motion causing the clubhead to dig into the ground beneath the ball. Also called **CHOP**.
2. To suddenly pull or twist the golf club during the swing.
3. An unpleasant personality.
4. To pull a shot left of its intended line of flight.

JEU DE MAIL:

A game with its origins in Italy, it was taken up by the French and became especially widespread in the early 17th century. It went out of fashion some 100 years later, but until 50 years ago, it remained a regular activity in southern France as Jeu De Mail La Chicane, a cross-country version of the game. The game has techniques very similar to golf, and it was played on a court prepared specifically for its play. It eventually arrived in England from France and its name was translated into pall mall.

JIGGER:
1. An archaic name for an iron with a narrow blade, the equivalent of today's 4-iron. Also called a **SAMMY**.
2. An obsolete club used for chip shots. Also called the **PITCHING WEDGE**.

JITTERS:
When a golfer feels extremely nervous.

JOY OF GOLF:
An expression of happiness and outward rejoicing in playing well. A strong feeling of pleasure arising from a sense of well being and happiness. Feeling pleasure from playing well.

JOY OF GOLF

JUDGMENT:
The golfer's ability to make a sound decision on how hard the ball should be hit for the distance needed and what club to use for the shot.

JUICE:
A reverse spin put on the ball to make it stop on the green or roll backward. It is the clockwise spinning action imparted on the ball by the face of the club. Also called an **ACTION, BITE, VAMPIRE, GROW TEETH, BICUSPID** or **OVERBITE**.

JUICY LIE:
A good lie in the fairway or rough.

JUNIOR:
Any golfer below the age of eighteen.

JUMP

JUNIOR TOURNAMENT:
Open to golfers below the age of eighteen. Usually played in stroke play format, 18 to 36 holes, with no handicap.

JUMP:
When the ball **JUMPS** off the clubface and travels farther than normal.

JUMP ON IT:
1. To take advantage of a situation.
2. To strike the ball with maximum power.

JUNGLE:

1. Very high and thick grass. Also called the **HEAVY ROUGH**.
2. Any punishing form of natural growth bordering fairways, such as trees, bushes, and weeds.
3. A tangled mess.

JUNGLE

JUNK:
A term for all golfing side bets. Referring to any side bets made by any golfer.

KEEPER:

A successful shot or score.

KEVLAR:

High impact plastic used in bulletproof vests. Also used occasionally for clubheads and mixed with graphite to make shafts.

KICK:

1. When you kick your ball into a better hitting position. Also called **KICKED THE BALL**.
2. Another term for bounce. Usually an unpredictable or erratic bounce.

KICKERS:

A golf tournament played with any number of golfers. The tournament committee draws a number, advising a player that it is, for example, between 70 and 80. Players select their own handicaps without knowing the number drawn. The player whose net score equals, or is closest to, the number drawn is the winner. This is a good type of tournament to schedule when accurate handicap information for a large percentage of the players is not available. Also called **KICKERS' TOURNAMENT**.

KICKERS' REPLAY:

A golf tournament played with any number of golfers. Each player is allowed to replay any (and only) two shots in a round. The player must continue with the replayed ball once it is called. The full handicap is used. Also called **KICKERS' REPLAY TOURNAMENT**.

KICK IN:

When a ball is so close to the hole, it is virtually impossible to miss it and it is given by the opposing player or team. It is counted as one stroke. Also called **DEAD** and **GIMMIE**.

KICK POINT:

A term used in golf shaft technology to pinpoint the flex point in a golf shaft. The lower the kick point, the higher the launch angle. A high **KICK POINT** means near the hands; low kick point indicates greater flex near the hosel.

KICK THE BALL:
When you kick your ball into a better hitting position. Also called **KICK**.

KIKUYU:
A fast-growing grass, common in California and mild climates, with thick, wiry blades that can wrap around, causing errant shots.

KICK THE BALL

KILL:
To hit a very long shot. Also called **KILL THE BALL**.

KINESIOLOGY:
The scientific study of mankind's movement and the movements of implements or equipment which he or she might use in exercise, sport, or other physical activity.

KINETIC ENERGY:
The form of energy associated with the speed of an object. Its equation is $KE = \ll mv2$; **or kinetic energy =1/2 mass x velocity squared**. It is obvious from the formula that increasing clubhead velocity has more potential for producing distance than increasing the clubhead weight.

KING OF THE HILL:
A golf game with any number of golfers. A player or team must make three pars in a row or better to be "KING". As soon as a bogey or more is made on a hole, you are no longer "KING". You must then make three more pars in a row to get to be "KING".

KITTY LITTER:
A term referring to a **SAND TRAP**. Also called **TRAP, BUNKER, SAND** and **BEACH**.

KNEE ACTION:
The inward motion of your knees in toward the ball during the swing. Your knees are a reliable index to correct footwork.

KNEE ACTION

KNEE FLEX:
A slight bend at the knees to reduce tension in your lower body, giving you a swinging balance.

KNEE KNOCKER:

A short putt, in the 2-to 5-foot range, that causes a golfer mental and physical anxiety. Also called a **YIPS PUTT**.

KNICKERS:

A type of trousers that reach to just below the knee. Also called **PLUS FOURS**.

KNIFE:

The hardest iron to use and hit with successfully. Referring to the **ONE IRON**. Also called **DRIVING IRON**.

KNOCKDOWN SHOT:

1. A shot with low trajectory usually played into the wind. Similar to the **PUNCH SHOT**.
2. A shot with a shortened backswing.

KNOCKOFF:

1. A copy of the original.
2. A club that is a clone of an original design.

KNUCKLE BALL:

A shot without spin that has an uncontrollable flight pattern.

KOLVEN:

A golflike Dutch game played in the 17th century.

KNICKERS

L P G A:
Ladies Professional Golf Association.

LADIES GAME:
Expression used to describe the dignity and respect for the game of golf. Also called the **GENTLEMENS GAME**.

LADIES TEES:
Tee areas and tee blocks placed somewhat closer to the green to compensate for distance. Usually indicated by red tee blocks.

LAG:
A long putt hit with intent of leaving the ball close to the cup. To play a putt to get close to, but short of, falling into the hole.

LAG PUTT:
A putt played so as to get close to, but short of, the hole.

LAG PUTTING:
The making of lag putts.

LAID BACK:
A clubface lofted, or tilted back, by the player to increase the effective loft.

LAID OFF:
When the club points to the left of the target at the top of the backswing.

LAMINATED:
A type of wood head made by gluing thin strips of maple together.

LARGE:
1. Expression used to describe a well-hit drive or long shot.
2. When a golfer is playing extremely well.

LATERAL HAZARD

LATE HIT:
The hinging of the wrists late in the downswing. The ball tends to travel to the right.

LATERAL HAZARD:
A water hazard marked by red stakes or lines. Water hazards that run parallel to the fairway, making it nearly impossible to drop the ball behind the hazard under normal rules. A ditch, stream, or pond roughly parallel to the line of the hole. When a ball lands in a **LATERAL HAZARD**, the player is penalized one stroke.

LATERAL SHIFT:
One of the movements of the body in the forward swing with the purpose of transferring the weight from over the right foot to over the left foot. It accompanies and can be the result of body rotation.

LATERAL SWAY:
The body center moving right and left throughout the golf swing.

LAUNCH ANGLE:
The angle at which the ball comes off the clubface immediately after impact.

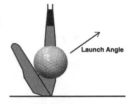

LAUNCHED:
A drive or long shot that takes off very well and flies for a great distance.

LAUNCH ANGLE

LAY:
To hit the ball or make a shot in a stated place by playing a stroke.

LAY BACK:
To tilt a clubface or clubhead back so as to increase its effective loft.

LAY OFF:
Flattening the plane at the top of the backswing, causing the club to point left of the target and the face to be closed. Literally "laying the clubhead down" so it is no longer square or on plane.

LAYOUT:
The manner in which the holes are placed on the golf course when designed. Also called **MAKE-UP OF A HOLE** and **HOLE MAKE UP**.

LAY UP:
Hitting a shot short on purpose because of trouble, such as a water hazard.

LEAD TAPE:
Adhesive tape backed with a thin layer of lead. Used to add weight to clubheads. The use of **LEAD TAPE** on the clubs is against the Rules of Golf.

LEAD TAPE

LEADER BOARD:
A place where the lowest scores in a tournament are posted.

LEADING EDGE:
The line between the clubface and the sole of the club which is used to help correct clubface aim.

LEAF RULE:
Some courses during autumn allow golfers to play another ball without penalty when his or her previous shot is lost and is assumed to be covered by leaves.

LEAK:
To fade undesirably to the right, as a shot does while flying toward the target. The ball glides slightly to the right during flight. For the right-handed golfer.

LEAK OIL:
1. When a golfer's game is falling to pieces and he/she is not playing well.
2. A golfer who is leading in a tournament but has, begun to give away shots and is beginning to lose.

LEANER

LEANER:
A shot that lies so close to the hole that it seems like half of the ball is hanging over the edge of the cup but does not fall in the hole.

LEARNING CENTER:
A complete golf practice and learning facility. Could include practice areas for full swing, short game, special shots such as uneven lies, putting, physical training, psychological training, equipment testing, video analysis, classroom, learning aids, and club fitting.

LEAST PUTTS:
This is a putting game. The player with the least number of putts wins. Count only the strokes taken on the putting surface.

LEFT EDGE - RIGHT EDGE:
The sides of the cup used as a target.

LEGS:
A ball is said to have legs if it continues to roll a long distance after landing. Also called **GET LEGS**.

**LEFT EDGE -
RIGHT EDGE**

LEG DRIVE:
The movement of the legs toward the target during the swing.

LENGTH:
1. Long hit.
2. The distance from the heel portion of the sole of the clubhead to the top of the grip.

LEVEL TURN:
Turning the shoulders level to the ground rather then tilting them up and down.

LEVER SYSTEM:
The skeletal system is composed of numerous bones which, in mechanical terms, act as levers. The two primary levers in the golf swing are;
1. The left arm, comprised of the radius and ulna of the lower arm and the humerus in the upper arm.
2. The club when the left wrist becomes cocked.

LIE:
1. The position in which the ball rests on the ground. It must be played from that point unless impossible or the rules state otherwise.
    A. <u>Good Lie</u>   - When the ball is sitting up well.
    B. <u>Bare Faced Lie</u> - When the ball sitting on a path or a worn down surface.
    C. <u>Bad Lie</u>   - When the ball is sitting in the rough, needles, divot, or some type similar of trouble.
    D. <u>Unplayable Lie</u> - Not being able to take a stroke on the ball.
    E. <u>Downhill Lie</u>   - Ball resting on a downhill slope.
    F. <u>Uphill Lie</u>   - Ball resting on an uphill slope.
    G. <u>Plugged Lie</u>   - Ball resting below the surface of the sand.
    H. <u>Embedded Lie</u>   - Ball buried in wet turf.

2. The angle formed by the centerline of the shaft and the ground when the clubhead is properly soled, with the clubface square to the target. Also called **LIE OF THE CLUB**.
3. Current number of strokes played on a hole.

LIE ALIKE:
An obsolete term meaning having played an equal number of strokes for a hole. Also called **LIKE AS WE LIE** and **LIKE AS THEY LIE**.

LIE ANGLE:
The angle at which the hosel and club shaft come away from the clubhead.

LIE ANGLE

LIE CLUB:
The lie of the ball which will indicate what kind of shot and club should be used.

LIE OF THE CLUB:
The angle the shaft makes with the clubhead as measured from the center of the shaft to a line extending tangentially from the lowest point on the sole.

LIFT:
The act of picking up the golf ball.

LIFT, CLEAN, AND PLACE:
To pick up the ball when playing in extremely wet conditions, clean the mud off, and replace it without penalty. The rule that goes into effect when the ball can easily become embedded in the course of normal play.

LIKE:
An obsolete expression used when the player has the same number of strokes for a hole as an opponent. Also called **TO PLAY THE LIKE**.

LIFT

LIKE AS WE LIE:
An obsolete term meaning having played an equal number of strokes for a hole. Also called **LIE ALIKE** and **LIKE AS THEY LIE**.

LINE:
Line, line of flight, or line of play all refer to the direction a golfer intends his or her ball to travel when it is hit.

LINE OF PLAY:
The direction the player wants the ball to travel from where it lies to the hole. The line you want the ball to follow after a stroke, with a reasonable distance added on either side of the intended line. The line of play extends vertically from the ground, but does not go beyond the hole.

LINE OF PUTT:
This is the line you want the ball to follow when you make contact with it on the putting green. The line of putt allows for a reasonable distance on either side of the intended path, but the line does not extend beyond the hole. The golfer cannot stand astride of or on the line of putt.

LINE UP:
To study the green in order to determine how the putt should be played.

LINING UP THE SHOT:
Aligning the body, ball, and swing to the intended target.

LINE OF PUTT

LINKS:
1. Any golf course can be called by this name. Also called **COURSE, GOLF COURSE** and **GREEN**.
2. Genuine links are found only adjacent to a seacoast where centuries of weathering have created turbulent sandy soil. Courses built in this type of terrain. Golf course within four miles of the coast.

LINKSLAND:
The seaside terrain typical of British courses.

LINKSMAN:
A golfer.

LIP:
The edge or rim of the cup or bunker.

LINKSMAN

LIP OUT:
When the ball touches the edge of the cup but does not fall in. Also refers to the **CELLOPHANE BRIDGE**.

LIZZY:
A shot that is a little **FAT** but is still okay and playable.

LOB SHOT:
A short golf shot which goes as high as it goes far, landing softly and under control. Very useful in circumstances where little green is available, a lob shot travels nearly straight up and down. It moves with very little over-spin or forward momentum.

LOB WEDGE:
A wedge with 60 degrees or more loft angle.

LOCAL KNOWLEDGE:
The advantage a player has competing on a course he or she knows.

LOB WEDGE

LOCAL RULES:
The rules of individual golf clubs printed on scorecards and read before a round. These are rules that are followed in addition to the official Rules of Golf. Set of rules determined by the members.

LOCK JAW:
When a golfer refuses to concede the closest of putts. Also called a **TIGHT WAD**.

LOFT:
   1. The height the ball reaches after being hit.
   2. The angle of the clubface. The amount in degrees that the clubface
      is angled.

LOFT MEASUREMENT:
   The precise measurement between the angle of the
clubface and the parallel line of the clubshaft.

LOFT
MEASUREMENT

LOFTIER:
   An obsolete highly lofted club that was the prede-
cessor of the niblick.

LOFTING MASHIE:
   An obsolete club used for playing a short lofting shot. The blade of the
club was laid back.

LONG AND WRONG:
   A golfer who hits the ball a great distance, but the direction of the shot
is always off the right or left of the intended line of flight.

LONG DRIVING:
   The making of long drives. Capable of long drives.

LONG GAME:
   That part of a golfer's game which involves hitting the ball over 180
yards. Shots taken with the woods and long irons.

LONG IRONS:
   The relatively straight-faced and long-hitting irons. Referring to the
1, 2, 3, and 4 irons.

LONG-SHORT TOURNEY:
   Many players have bad long games and good short games, and vice
versa. This event combines the abilities of these two types of golfers.
One player does the driving and long shot making and his or her partner does the approaching and putting. Players usually select their own
playing partners.

LOOP:
   1. A change in the path of the clubhead during the swing.
   2. The shape of the arc the clubhead makes when the backswing and
      forward swing planes don't match. If the forward swing plane is
      under (flatter than) the backswing plane, it is an inside loop. If the
      forward swing plane is over (steeper than) the backswing plane, it
      is an outside loop.
   3. Caddie slang for a round of golf.

LOOPER:
Another name for the **CADDIE**.

LOOPING:
A backswing fault in which the head and shoulder of the golfer move forward and to the left so that they extend over the ball more than what is correct. This makes the clubhead return to the ball from the outside causing the golfer to shank the ball.

LOOSE IMPEDIMENT:
Natural objects such as stones, leaves, twigs, branches, worms, insects, and the like that obstruct play -- as long as they are not fixed or growing, are not solidly embedded, and do not adhere to the ball. Sand and loose soil are loose impediments on the putting green only. Snow and natural ice (other than frost) can be either casual water or loose impediments. Manufactured ice is an obstruction. Dew and frost are not loose impediments. Loose impediments can be removed without penalty as long as the ball is not in motion and the loose impediment and the ball do not lie in (or touch) a hazard. Loose impediments cannot be moved if a ball is in motion, even if the loose impediment may influence the movement of the ball. In a hazard, if the ball is covered by loose impediments or sand, the player can only remove enough debris to allow him/her to see the ball.

LOOSENED GRIP:
Any time during the swing when a player opens his fingers on the grip to cause some loss of control. The most common example would be opening the last three fingers of the left hand at the top of the backswing. Also called a **PICCOLO GRIP**.

LOOSENED GRIP

LOST BALL:
Self explanatory. The rules allow you five minutes to find a lost ball. If after that time it is still not found, you have to put another ball into play, following the rules, without searching for the original ball. You have resumed play with a provisional ball. In this case, the provisional ball becomes the ball in play if the original ball is not found. Also called **BALL LOST**.

LOTS OF GAME:
1. A golfer who is excellent in all phases of the game.
2. When there are a lot of holes remaining to be played in the tournament or round.

LOW BALL:

1. Used when referring to the best ball in a group of players that has the lowest score on the hole.
2. It is a four-ball match with handicap strokes.
3. In this golf game, each hole is given a predetermined value. The player with the low ball on each hole wins the predetermined points for that hole. If the hole is tied, no points are awarded. The player with the most points wins.

LOW BALL AND TOTAL:

A four ball team bet where the best ball of each team wins a point and the lowest total of the partners wins another point.

LOW FINISH:

A follow-through that stops, deliberately or otherwise, shorter than normal, as in the **PUNCH SHOT**.

LOW HANDICAPPER:

A good golfer who receives a low number of handicap strokes such as under ten.

LOW NET FOURSOME:

The total score of four players, less handicaps, determines the winning foursome in the field of players.

LOW NET PLUS PUTTS:

In this golf game, each player keeps score for each hole and keeps track of all putts. At the end of play, the handicap is subtracted, then putts added to the net score. The player with the lowest score wins.

LOW SIDE:

The area below the hole on a sloping green. Also called **AMATEUR SIDE**.

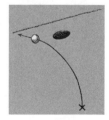

LOW SIDE

LUCK IT:

To drop a putt which the player did not think was well hit.

LURKING:

A golfer who is in position to make a move toward the top of the leader board.

MAJORS:
The most significant golf championships. They include: The Masters, the U.S. Open, the British Open, and the PGA Championship. Also called the **MAJOR TOURNAMENTS**.

MAKABLE:
A shot with a good chance of being made.

MAKE:
1. To hole a shot.
2. An obsolete term meaning to play a round or course in a stated number of strokes.

MAKE THE CUT:
To qualify for the two final rounds of a 72-hole tournament by scoring well enough in the first two rounds.

MAKE THE TURN:
Starting the back nine after finishing the front nine.

MALLET PUTTER:
A putter with a wide head.

MALLET PUTTER

MARK:
1. To indicate the position of the ball with a small round object.
2. To identify the spot on the green where a player has lifted up a ball for cleaning purposes or to clear the way for another putt.

MARKER:
1. A small round object placed behind the ball to indicate the position of the ball before you lifted it.
2. Anyone the committee appoints to record a competitor's score in stroke play. This person can be a fellow competitor, but is not considered a referee.
3. An object that determines the forward limits from which to drive. Also called **TEE BLOCKS, MARKERS** and **TEE MARKERS**.

MARKERS:
An object that determines the forward limits from which to drive. Also called **TEE BLOCKS**.

MARK

MARSHALL:
The person controlling the crowd at tournaments.

MASHIE:
An iron club with a short head introduced in the 1880's.
A lofted iron club, no longer in use, introduced about
1880 and used for pitching with backspin. In its day,
this hickory-shafted club was a favored iron of many
golfers, used for practically everything. Also called
the **FIVE IRON**.

MARSHALL

MASHIE IRON:
A heavier mashie with a somewhat longer shaft than a mashie. An iron
club, no longer in use, somewhat less lofted than a mashie, that was
used for driving and for full shots through the green. Also the **FOUR
IRON**.

MASHIE NIBLICK:
An iron club, no longer in use, having a loft between those of a mashie
and a **NIBLICK**, used for pitching. Also called the **SIX IRON** or **SEVEN
IRON**.

MASTERS:
The first major tournament of each calendar year. It is always played at
the Augusta National course in Georgia. Also called the **MASTER
TOURNAMENT**.

MATCH:
A golf "match" is a competition between two or more golfers. Both
medal and match play can constitute a match.

MATCHED:
1. A group of players in a foursome.
2. Individual player being asked to join the twosome or threesome by
   the starter.
3. A set of matching clubs.

MATCH OF CARDS:
A way to break ties by comparing the scorecards, with the lower score
on a particular hole winning the match.

MATCH

MATCH PLAY:
A golf game in which the score is decided by holes won or lost. Competition by the number of holes played; the player or team winning the most holes is the winner of the match. Tied holes have no effect on the score. A hole is won when a team or player holes out the ball in fewer strokes than their opponent.

MATCH PLAYER:
A golfer considered in terms of ability at match play rather than stroke play.

MATCHED SET:
Clubs designed and made in a graded, numbered series and with consistent specifications and swing weight. Also called **MATCHED**.

MATCHED SET

MEADOWLAND:
A lush grassland course.

MEAT AND POTATOES:
1. A straightforward hole with no hazards to play around or over.
2. A type of shot or shots that have been mastered by a player.
3. A golfer's favorite and most consistent shot. Also called **BREAD AND BUTTER**.

MECHANICS:
The technique elements a player selects and employs in making a golf shot.

MEDAL:
Medal refers to medal play or a medal awarded to a champion or medalist. Do not confuse "medal" with "medalist." A medalist is the low scorer in the qualifying round of a tournament.

MEDALIST:
A medalist is the individual who has the lowest qualifying score for a tournament.

MEDAL DAY:
A calendar day during which you are entitled to play a medal round in a competition.

MEDAL PLAY:
A golf game in which the score is decided by the total strokes taken and the player with the lowest total is the winner. Competition by the total overall score. The player or team with the fewest strokes for the stipulated round wins the match. To determine each player's or team's score, the total number of strokes for each hole is calculated and then the appropriate deductions for any handicap(s) are made. Also called **MEDAL ROUND** and **STROKE PLAY**.

MEMBERS BOUNCE:
   A lucky bounce that makes the player look like he/
   she knew what they where doing the whole time.

METAL WOOD:
   A wooden club made out of metal.

MICKEY MOUSE COURSE:
   1. A poorly maintained golf course.
   2. An extremely easy course that offers no challenge to the golfer.

METAL WOOD

MID IRON:
   An iron head club for medium distances, having less loft than a **CLEEK**
   or **DRIVING IRON** and more than a **MASHIE**. An iron club, no longer
   in use, somewhat more lofted than a driving iron. Also called a **ONE
   IRON** or **TWO IRON**.

MID MASHIE:
   A deep faced mashie with a slightly longer shaft than a **MASHIE**.
   Also called the **THREE IRON**.

MID SPOON:
   An obsolete wooden club with a loft between that
   of the spoon and the short iron.

MIDDLE IRONS:
   The middle irons are the 5, 6 and 7 irons.

MIDDLE IRONS

MIDDLE WEDGE:
   A club for producing medium loft, approximately between that of a
   pitching wedge and a sand wedge.

MILITARY GOLF:
   A slang term for a person who hits a ball to the right, then one to the
   left, etc., from "Left, Right, Right, Left." Also called **ARMY GOLF**.

MILKING THE GRIP:
   To tighten or lighten the grip on the club before taking the shot. Also
   called **FEELING THE GRIP**.

MILLION DOLLAR SWING:
   A flawless swing.

MIS-ABLE:
   A putt or shot somewhat challenging and understand
   if missed.

MIS-CLUB:
   Choosing the wrong club for the shot to be taken.

MIS-HIT:
   Any shot that is not hit on the center of the club face.

MILITARY GOLF

MIS-READ:
To take the wrong line on a putt. To putt wrongly.

MIXED FOURSOME:
Two men and two women in any combination.

MODEL SWING:
The ideal swing or motion. Mastering the swing.

MIXED FOURSOME

MODULAS:
An expression used to indicate the quality in a graphite shaft. The higher the **MODULAS,** the richer the fibers and therefore a more stronger and consistent shaft.

MOVED:
Any time a ball leaves its position and comes to rest in another place, it is considered to have moved. Also called **MOVE.**

MONDAY'S CHILDREN:
Pros who compete on Monday morning in an attempt to earn entry into that week's tournament.

MONEY MAKER:
1. A golfer who makes a great deal of money playing golf.
2. A golfer who seems to make every important shot or putt.

MOST LIKELY SCORE:
The score a player shall post for handicap purposes when he starts but does not complete a hole or is conceded. This number may not exceed the player's **EQUITABLE STROKE CONTROL** limit.

MUFF:
To mis-hit a shot.

MULLIGAN:
A second attempt at a shot, usually played off the first and tenth tees, although the number can be agreed upon by players before the round begins. This is illegal and against the Rules of Golf. When an American golfer hit his first tee shot into the woods and teed up another ball, he told his Scottish caddie that, "In America, we call this taking a mulligan." The caddie replied, "In Scotland, we call that hitting three." Also called **SHAPIRO.**

MUNICIPAL COURSE:
A golf course owned by the government and open to the public.

MUNICIPAL COURSE

MUSCLE MEMORY:
Automatic habit of the correct swing movements developed by disciplined and repetitive practice.

NAP:
1. The direction in which the grass has been cut. Also called the **GRAIN**.
2. The way the grass is growing and at what angle.

NARROW FOCUS:
Mentally honing in as tightly as possible on the target while blocking out unnecessary thoughts and distractions.

NASSAU:
A three-part bet in which a round of 18 holes is divided into three separate wagers - front nine, back nine, and full eighteen.

NASSAU TOURNAMENT:
Similar to the handicap stroke play, except that handicap strokes are taken hole by hole as they fall on the card. Prizes are awarded for the best score on the front nine, the best score on the back nine and the best overall score for all eighteen holes.

NASTY:
A bet that is won when a shot from off the putting green is holed and your score on that hole is par or better. Also called **WATSON** and **CRENSHAW**.

NATIONAL GOLF FOUNDATION:
One of leading sources of research and information for golf industry. They foster the growth and economic vitality of golf. Also called **NGF**.

NATURAL:
1. A birdie made without the aid of any handicap strokes.
2. A player who seems to makes shots without having to practice and play much.

NEAREST POINT OF RELIEF:
The point no nearer the hole that is the closest point where relief may be taken. Ball moved for relief but the ball is not advanced towards the hole.

NECK:
The tapered projecting part where the shaft of the club joins the head. Also called **HOSEL**.

NECK

NECK

NEEDLE:
1. Trying to talk your opponent into making an extra bet or causing him to over try.
2. Describes the making of an extra bet at an even point in a match.

NEEDLE LIE:
When the ball is resting on pine needles.

NEGATIVE ACCELERATION:
A negative change in the velocity of a moving object. In golf it usually refers to decreasing clubhead speed. It is a major error when occurring prior to impact. Also called **DECELERATION** and **QUITTING**.

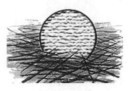

NEEDLE LIE

NET SCORE:
Your score at the end of the round after deducting your handicap. Also called **NET**.

NEUTRAL GRIP:
A way of gripping the club so the hands will return to the same position at impact, usually parallel to the clubface.

NEVER UP, NEVER IN:
Term of criticism for putting short of the hole.

NGF:
One of leading sources of research and information for golf industry. They foster the growth and economic vitality of golf. Also called **NATIONAL GOLF FOUNDATION**.

NIBLICK:
A deep-bladed iron club, no longer in use, developed from the earlier iron niblick, more steeply lofted than a mashie, used especially for playing from sand and from rough. This club was introduced by Lord Niblick of England in 1862. Also called the **NINE IRON**.

NINE:
A sequence of nine holes or a nine-hole golf course.

NINES:
This is a three-player game. The object is to get as many points as possible. There are nine points awarded on each hole. Decide the value of each point before the game begins. Also called **NINE**.
The point system is as follows:
    5 points for low ball
    3 points for 2nd low ball
    1 point for the last place
         or
    4 points for two who tie for low ball
    1 point for last place
         or
    5 points for low ball
    2 points for two who tie for 2nd low ball
         or
    3 points for a three-way tie

NEUTRAL GRIP

NINE IRON:
An iron club having loft of 45-48 degrees, lie of 62-64 degrees, and length of 35 inches. Giving distances of 120-150 yards for the men and 95-125 yards for the ladies. Also called a **NIBLICK**.

NINETEENTH HOLE:
Refers to the clubhouse bar.

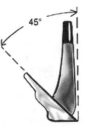

NINETY DEGREE RULE:
Golf cart restrictions that allow carts to enter and exit fairways only on a 90-degree angle.

NIP IT:

NINE IRON

When a player takes an iron shot without taking a divot it produces less backspin than normal.

NO BLOOD:
When a hole was halved, or played to a tie and money was won or lost.

NON-SELECTIVE PERIMETER WEIGHTING:
Equal weight over the toe and heel of the clubhead.

NOSE:
The toe of a club.

NUKED:
A shot that has achieved its maximum distance.

NINETY DEGREE
RULE

OB :
Abbreviation for **OUT OF BOUNDS**. Also called **OSCAR BRAVO, SET IT FREE** and **OSCAR BROWN**.

OBSERVER:
An individual appointed by the committee to help the referee decide questions of fact and to report any breach of a rule to the referee. An observer should not attend the flagstick, stand at or mark the position of the hole, or lift the ball or mark its position. The committee can appoint anyone to be an observer.

OBSTACLE FACTORS:
The evaluation of ten factors on the golf course on a scale of 1 to 10, considering separately their effect on the play of scratch and bogey golfers. They are as follows:
1. Topography
2. Fairways
3. Green Target
4. Recoverability and Rough
5. Bunkers
6. Out of Bounds
7. Water hazards
8. Trees
9. Putting surface
10. Psychological

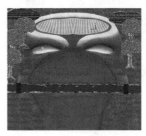

OBSTRUCTIONS

OBSTRUCTIONS:
Anything artificial, including the artificial surfaces and sides of roads and paths, that interferes with play. Manufactured ice is also considered an obstruction. Some artificial items are not considered obstructions, including:
1. Objects defining out of bounds, such as walls, fences, stakes, and railings.
2. Any part of an immovable artificial object that is out of bounds.
3. Any construction declared by the committee to be an integral part of the course. The committee decides whether or not you can get relief from an artificial object considered to be an integral part of the course.

ODD OR ODDS:
An obsolete term meaning a stroke that brings one's score for a hole to one more than that of one's opponent. Being one stroke or hole up on your opponent.

OFF-CENTER HIT:
Hitting the ball not in the center of the face.

OFF GREEN:
A style of chipping which uses a low-to-medium trajectory club in a distinctly putting-like style. Using the special club called the **CHIP-PER**.

OFF SET:
A club with the head set behind the shaft. A club with a head that is set back from the hosel, putting the hands further in front to help square the club at impact.

ON:
1. On or onto the putting greens.
2. Playing well.

ON FIRE:
When a golfer is playing consistently well.

ON IN ONE:
Landing on the green from the tee.

ON LINE:
Swinging the clubhead through the target line.

ONE IRON

ON THE CLOCK:
A warning to slow playing golfers. When a group of slow playing professionals are informed by tournament officials that their play will be timed to ensure it is within the rules and continued slow play will result in a penalty.

ON THE DANCE FLOOR:
When the ball has stayed on the green. An expression indicating that the ball is on the putting green.

ON THE SCREWS:
Expression used to describe a well executed wood shot.

ONE A SIDE:
When your opponent insists that his or her handicap is two strokes higher than yours, so you give him or her a stroke on the most difficult hole on each nine - **ONE A SIDE**.

ONE IRON:
An iron club having loft of about 17-18 degrees, lie of about 56 degrees, length of 39 inches, and giving distance of 195-250 yards for the men and 175-205 yards for the ladies. Also called **DRIVING IRON**.

ONE PIECE:

The early portion of the backswing in which the arms, hands and wrists move away from the ball in nearly the same relation to each other as they were at address. The wrists may hinge very slightly.

ONE PUTT:

Holing the ball in one putt.

ONE SHOT:

A hole requiring one good drive to reach the green.

ONE SHOTTER:

1. One-shot to the putting surface.
2. A par three hole

ONE UP:

1. Leading by one stroke.
2. In match play, describing a player or a team that has won one more hole than his opponent.

ONE WOOD

ONE WOOD:

A wooden club having loft of 11 to 12-1/2 degrees, the lie of 54-56 degrees, length of 43 inches. Giving distances of 200-350 yards for the men and 195-275 yards for the ladies. Also called **DRIVER** and **PLAY CLUB**.

OPEN:

A tournament in which both amateurs and professionals are allowed to play. Also called **OPEN TOURNAMENT**.

OPEN FACE 1

OPEN FACE GRIP:

An exaggerated counterclockwise rotational positioning of the hands when placed on the club. Also **WEAK GRIP**.

OPEN FACE:

1. The club face aligned to the right of the target at address. Whenever the angle formed by the leading edge of the clubface is greater than 90 degrees to the tangent of the swing arc. Also called **OPEN CLUBFACE**.
2. Tilting the clubhead back with more of the face pointing skyward.

OPEN FACE 2

OPEN SETUP:
The act of aligning oneself left of the intended target with your position at address.

OPEN STANCE:
When the left foot is drawn back from the intended line of flight, and turning your body slightly towards the hole. This type of stance encourages a slice.

OPEN STANCE

OPEN THE DOOR:
When a golfer begins to play poorly and allows his or her opponent back into the hole, match, or tournament.

OPEN TO CLOSED:
A description of the dynamics of the clubhead when the player rolls the face open during the backswing and rolls it closed during the forward swing. Also called **OPEN TO SHUT**.

OPEN UP THE HOLE:
When your tee shot leaves the best possible angle for the next shot to the green.

ORDER OF PLAY:
1. The golfer with the **HONOR** on the tee.
2. The player who is **AWAY** is to play next.
3. The committee dictates the order of play off the first tee in a tournament competition.

OPEN TO CLOSED

OUT:
The first nine holes of an 18-hole golf course. Also called the **FRONT NINE, OUTWARD NINE** or **OUTWARD HALF**.

OUT OF BOUNDS:
Specially laid out areas on the golf course are out of bounds. Usually marked by white posts. Also called **OSCAR BRAVO, SET IT FREE, OB** and **OSCAR BROWN**.

OUT OF BOUNDS SHOT:
Stroke that comes to rest in an out of bounds area. Shot must be taken from the original position, thus sacrificing distance gained, with one penalty stroke added.

OUTSIDE AGENCY:
Anyone who is not part of the competitor's side in stroke play or not of the match.

OUTSIDE THE LINE:
The area on the opposite side of the intended target line as a player addresses the ball and swings.

OUTSIDE TO IN:
The swing path of the clubhead when it arrives from outside the target line traveling across the ball and then moves inside the line immediately after impact. The forward swing plane with this pattern is invariably steeper than the backswing plane. Also called **OUT TO IN** and **OUT AND IN**.

OUTWARD NINE:
The first nine holes of the round. Also the **FRONT, FIRST NINE, FRONT NINE, OUTWARD HALF** and **OUT**.

OVERLAPPING GRIP:
A type of grip where the little finger of the left hand lies over the index finger of the right hand.

OVERCLUB:
Using a club that will hit the ball farther than the target.

OVERCOOK IT:
1. To hit a shot too hard.
2. To place too much hooking or slicing spin on the ball.

OVERLAPPING
GRIP

OVER AND BACK:
To hit an approach shot over the green and on the next shot shoot over the green again.

OVERBITE:
A spin that makes the ball tend to stop rather than roll when it lands. Also called **VAMPIRE, BITE, BICUSPID** or **BACKSPIN**.

OVER GOLF:
To play an excessive amount of golf.

OVER PAR:
A score higher than the indicated par for a hole or round.

OVERRIDE:
A **HANDICAP COMMITTEE** action which cancels a **TOURNAMENT SCORE**.

OVER SWING:
1. Taking too long of a backswing needed for the shot.
2. Swinging the club in an uncontrolled manner.

OUTSIDE TO IN

OVER THE TOP:
The premature movement of the upper torso that sends the clubhead forward into an out-to-in swing path.

PACE:
1. The rate of movement in the swing.
2. The speed of the greens.

PADDLE GRIP:
The grip on a putter that has a flat surface along the top on which the player may rest his thumbs.

PAINT JOB:
1. A professional's putt that **LIPS OUT** because of the paint on the edge of the hole.
2. The paint around the hole's edge to make it easier for TV viewers to see their location.

PAIR:
1. Two golfers playing together in a stroke competition.
2. To assign players to play together in competition.

PAIRING:
The grouping of two golfers to play together in a stroke competition. Groups of two players. Also called **MATCHED**.

PAR:
The number of shots a scratch player is expected to take on any given hole on a course.

PAR CHART:
The par of each hole is decided by its length alone and not by its difficulty. It is based on yardage and two putts per green.

THE STANDARD PAR DISTANCE GUIDE		
PAR	MEN'S	WOMEN'S
3	Up to 250	Up to 210
4	251 to 470	211 to 400
5	471 to 575	401 to 500
6	576 and over	501 and over

PAR CHART

PAR FOR A PARTNER:
Golf game played in a threesome. Use par or bogey for the odd player's partner's score. Also called **PHANTOM PRO**.

PAR SHOOTER:
A golfer who shoots par most of the time.

PARALLEL:
The desired position at the top of the swing, with the clubshaft parallel to the ground. Also called **HORI-ZONTAL**.

PARALLEL LINES

PARALLEL LINES:
Lines which extend in the same direction. Example: Railroad tracks.

PARKLAND:
A course laid out in grassland with little rough.

PARTNER:
1. Player teamed with another golfer on the same side.
2. A player on your side.

PATH:
The directional arc in which the club is swung when viewed from above. Usually identified in the swing zone just prior to and after impact.

PAWKY:
Old Scottish term meaning cunning or tricky.

PEER REVIEW:
The process of allowing golfers the opportunity to play against one another and review each other's scoring records and USGA Handicap Indexes.

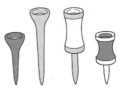

PEG

PEG:
A pin of wood or plastic driven into the ground to hold the ball on the **TEEING GROUND**. Also called a **TEE**.

PENAL:
The difficulty of a golf course. The architecture designed primarily to punish poor shots or poor shooters.

PENALTY:
1. In **STROKE PLAY**, A rule infringement costing one or two strokes, meaning the player adds one or two strokes to your overall score depending on the infringement.
2. In **MATCH PLAY**, the hole is usually lost.

PENALTY SCORE:
A score imposed upon a player by the USGA Handicap System for failing to return a score or follow the rules of the USGA Handicap System.

PENALTY STROKE:
A stroke added to players score for violation of the rules.

PENCIL BAG:
A small and thin golf bag used to lighten the load. Also called **SUMMER BAG**.

PENCIL KEEPER:
The golfer who keeps the score for the group. Also called **PENCIL HOCKEY**.

PENDULUM STROKE

PENDULUM STROKE:
A free swing from a fixed pivot point. In putting, a pure pendulum stroke could be with the hands and club swinging from the wrist joint while the arms are stabilized. A more common form is to use the arms and shoulders with the pivot point in the center of the chest.

PEORIA HANDICAP SYSTEM:
The **GOLF COMMITTEE** selects par 3, 4 and 5 holes on each nine. The amount over par on the selected holes is multiplied by 3 and this equals the handicap to be deducted. Maximum score is a **DOUBLE PAR**.

PERIMETER WEIGHTING:
Perimeter Weighting is typical among metal woods and most newer club sets. A majority of the weight of the club is moved to the toe and heel of the clubhead. This effectively expands the **SWEET SPOT** of the club, offering better off-center shots. Also called **CAVITY BACK CLUB**.

PERSIMMON:
A type of wood from which many wooden clubs are made.

PGA:
Professional Golfers' Association.

PERIMETER WEIGHTING

PGA TOUR:
The Professional Golfers' Association tournament circuit. Players must attend qualifying school or **Q-SCHOOL** to obtain their card, which allows them to play the tour for one year.

PICCOLO GRIP:
A very loose hold on the club, especially at the top of the backswing. Also called **LOOSENED GRIP**.

PICK AND DROP:
The act of lifting the ball up and dropping it in another spot as allowed by the rules in specified circumstances.

PICK IT:
To hit the ball and make little or no contact with the ground.

PICK IT UP:
To concede a putt.

PICK UP:
1. To lift up one's ball before holing out.
2. In match play, this concedes the hole.
3. In stroke play, this results in disqualification.

PICCOLO GRIP

PICKER:
A player who sweeps the ball off the ground with a flatter swinging path. Opposite of a **DIGGER**.

PIGEON:
An opponent you should beat easily.

PILL:
Nickname for the **BALL**.

PIN PLACEMENT

PIN:
The flag pole placed in hole. Recommended dimensions for a pin are seven feet high and three-quarters inches in diameter. Also called the **FLAGSTICK, FLAG POLE** and **FLAG**.

PIN HIGH:
When the ball rests on either side of the flag. Also called **FLAG HIGH** and **HOLE HIGH**.

PIN PLACEMENT:
The location of the flagstick and hole on the green. Also called **PIN POSITION** and **POSITION OF THE FLAG**.

PIN SEEKER:
A shot that heads straight for the flagstick the moment it leaves the clubface. Also called a **FLAG MISSILE** or **MISSILE**.

PIN SETTER:
The person responsible for **PIN PLACEMENT**.

PINCH SHOT:
A short shot around the green, struck with a crisp, descending blow. Most full iron shots, when struck a descending blow, are pinched to some degree. Similar to the **PUNCH SHOT**.

PINEHURST:
A variation of play in which a partner plays the other partner's drive. One ball is then selected to finish the hole.

PIPELINE:
The center of the fairway.

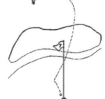

PITCHSHOT

PISTOL GRIP:
The grip portion on the handle of a putter which has extra build up at the top so that it fits the hand similarly to a small pistol handle.

PITCH:
To lob or loft a ball into the air onto or toward the green.

PITCH AND PUTT:
A short golf course designed primarily for approaching and putting.

PITCH AND RUN SHOT:
A shot that clears obstacles in the way of the green and rolls toward the hole.

PITCH MARK:
The indentation left on the green after the ball hits. It is important to fix the indentation so no one has to putt over it.

PITCH SHOT:
A shot that enables the golfer to clear hazards in the way of the green. There is not a lot of roll after landing. It is a high trajectory shot.

PITCHER:
The eight iron.

PITCH AND RUN SHOT

PITCHING:
Playing short shots to the green with a wedge or highly lofted club.

PITCHING IRONS:
The short irons PW, LW and SW.

PITCHING NIBLICK:
Old term for a **PITCHING WEDGE**.

PITCHING IRONS

PITCHING WEDGE:
An iron club used primarily for playing pitches to the green, having loft of 50-52 degrees, lie of 63-65 degrees, and length of about 35 inches, and having a flange less prominent than that of the sand wedge behind and below the leading edge, to prevent the clubhead from digging into grass. Giving distances of 85-140 yards for the men and 75-125 yards for the ladies. Used to hit a pitch shot. Also called **WEDGE**.

PIVOT:
The rotation of the body during the golf swing. The movement of the body or a body part around a fixed axis. Most commonly used to describe the body turn around the spine in the full backswing. Also referred to as **SHOULDER TURN, WINDUP** and **COIL**.

PLACEMENT:
Accuracy in the targeting of a shot.

PLANE:
The arc of the swing. Also called **SWING PLANE** and **SWINGING ARC**.

PLANE

PLATE:
YARDAGE MARKERS that are imbedded into the fairway indicating the distance to the center of the green. Also called **PLATE MARKERS** and **YARDAGE MARKERS**.
RED PLATE: 100 yards to the center of the green.
WHITE PLATE: 150 yards to the center of the green.
BLUE PLATE: 200 yards to the center of the green.

PLATEAU GREEN:
Greens that sit up much higher than the level of the fairway.

PLAY:
To strike the ball with a club. Also called **HIT**.

PLAY CLUB:
An ancient driver.

PLATEAU GREEN

PLAY-OFF:
Where two or more players play extra holes to break a tie.

PLAY'EM DOWN:
To play the ball as it lies.

PLAYABLE:
A ball lying so that it can be played.

PLAYABILITY:
A course with adequate quality to offer satisfactory play.

PLUGGED BALL

PLAYING HANDICAP:
The Exact Handicap rounded to the nearest whole number.

PLAYING ORDER:
1. The golfer with the **HONOR** on the tee.
2. The player who is **AWAY** is to play next.
3. The committee dictates the order of play off the first tee in a tournament competition. Also called **ORDER OF PLAY**.

PLAYING PARTNER:
A golfer playing in a partnership or on the same team as another. Also called **PARTNER**.

PLAYING PROFESSIONAL:
A professional golfer who primarily competes in tournaments.

PLAYING THROUGH:
When the group in front of you invites you to pass and play the hole before them. Passing ahead of players who are playing slow or who have halted play. Common courtesy dictates that you allow those playing behind you to play through if you are playing at a slower pace than they are, or if you have halted play for some reason such as when looking for a lost ball.

PLUGGED BALL:
A ball is plugged if it remains in its own pitch mark after hitting the green, bunkers or fairways. Plugged balls occur more often in wet conditions.

PLUMB BOB:
A system of lining up a putt.

PLUMB BOB

PLUS FOURS:
Style of knickers popularized by the 1920's golfers. Named for the additional four inches of fabric draped over the knee. Also called **KNICKERS**.

PLUS HANDICAP:
The number of strokes granted to adjust a golfer's score to the level of a scratch or better. For example, if a golfer shoots under par (if par is 72 and he is good enough to shoot 70 consistently), his handicap would be plus two.

PLUS MAN:
A man with a handicap better than scratch.

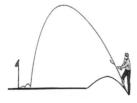

PLUS FOURS

POA ANNUA:
A weedlike grass found on many courses in the cooler spring months before dying out in the summer heat.

POINT:
A betting unit on any given hole.

POINT OF CONTACT:
The spot on the clubface that strikes the center of the ball.

POLE ONE:
To hit a long shot.

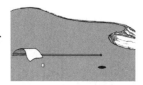

POLIE

POLEY:
An approach shot with an iron that ends up within the length of the flagstick.

POND BALL:
1. A golf ball intended for shots over water. Also called **WATER BALL**.
2. Beat up balls that are intended to be used to shoot over water. Also called **WATER BALL**.
3. Ball shot into the water. Also called **WATER BALL** and **DEPTH CHARGE**.

POP UP:
A high and short shot. Also called **POP**.

POSITION A:
The ideal position to attack the flag. The place that makes your next shot easy or easier.

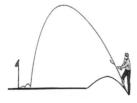

POP UP

POST:
To record your score for the day.

POSTING SHEET:
The document that is used to record your score for the day.

POSTURE:
The placement of the body at address. Also called **POSTURE AT ADDRESS** and **ADDRESS**.

POSTURE AT ADDRESS:
The position of your body at address. Also called **ADDRESS**.

POT:
A repository for the funds to be dispersed to people who win the game.

POT BUNKER:
A small and steeply faced bunker.

POWER:
The amount of force with which a golf ball is struck.

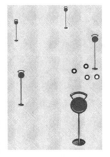

PRACTICE AIDS

PRACTICE AIDS:
Devices - videos, swing trainers, special clubs, etc. - designed to make practice more worthwhile and productive.

PRACTICE GREEN:
A place for working on your putting skills at the golf course.

PRACTICE TEE:
A place to practice drives.

PREFERRED LIE:
Used in the winter months so as not to damage the fairway. This rule permits you to move your ball to a position where you are less likely to take a divot or damage the fairways.

PRACTICE GREEN

PRE-SHOT ROUTINE:
A procedure which the player completes after selecting a club, but prior to starting the swing.

PRESIDENT:
An iron club, no longer in use, having steep loft equivalent to that of a **NIBLICK,** with a hole through the face, that was used for playing out of water.

PRESIDENT'S CUP:
A competition between the male professional golfers of the United States and the "rest of the world", except Europe, held every four years.

PRESS:
1. An extra bet made in the middle of a match, usually when a team or player is down by two holes. A press does not increase a bet it adds a new bet.
2. To attempt to hit the ball harder than usual or try harder than normal.

PREVAILING WIND:
The force and direction of the wind and its effect on the playing difficulty on the golf course.

PRIORITY ON THE COURSE:
Determining the order of play. Example: A single player must give way to a match consisting of 2, 3, or 4 players.

PRIVATE CLUB:
A club open to members and their guests only.

PRIVATE LESSON:
An instructional session which includes one pupil with one or more teachers.

PRO:
A professional golfer.

PRO AM:
A competition in which professional golfers team up with amateurs.

PRO SHOP:
A retail outlet where golf equipment, clothing, and other related items are for sale. Pro shops are frequently operated by a golf club's professional golfer. Also called **GOLF SHOPS**.

PROFESSIONAL:
A golfer who plays for a livelihood.

PRONATION:
An inward rotation of the hands toward the body's centerline when standing in a palms-facing-forward position. The term pronation was inaccurately used for many years to describe the rotation of both hands through the impact area. In fact, one hand, the right, was pronating while the left was supinating. It is impossible to pronate both hands through the shot.

PRO'S SIDE OF THE CUP:

The side above the hole when the cup is cut on a sloping green, since the professional usually allows for the slope better than the amateur. Also called **HIGH SIDE** and **PRO SIDE**.

PRO'S TEES:

The teeing ground located the farthest distance from the hole, used by the better players. Also called **BACK, BACK TEE, CHAMPIONSHIP TEE** and **TIGER TEES**.

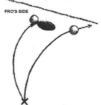

**PRO'S SIDE
OF THE CUP**

PROVISIONAL BALL:

The ball played after losing the one you just shot and lost. Also called **PROVISIONAL**.

PSYCHOLOGICAL:

The mental effect a player creates by the presence of an obstacle or combination of difficult obstacles in a target area.

PUBLIC COURSE:

A course open to the public. Also called **PUBLIC LINKS**.

PULL:

The flight of the ball straight, but to the left of the intended line of flight. Not as disastrous as the hook.

PULL CART:

A cart used to carry your golf bag around the course. Many clubs have pull carts and/or electric carts for rent. Also called a **TWO WHEELER** and **BUGGY**.

PULLED HOOK:

A hook which starts to the left of the target and curves even farther to the left.

PULL

PULLED SHOT:

A shot that travels on a relatively straight path, but to the left of the target.

PULLED SLICE:

A shot that starts out left of the target line and curves back to the extreme right.

PULL

PUNCH:
Controlled low shot.

PUNCHBOWL:
A putting green that sits in a hollow.

PUNCH SHOT:
A shot that keeps the ball low in very strong head winds.

PUNCH SHOT

PUSH :
A ball that flies straight to the right for a right-handed golfer.

PUSHED:
1. This is also another word for a tie. If two players halve a hole, the hole is said to be "pushed." Also called **HALVED** or **HALVE**.
2. When the group or groups of golfers that are behind you are waiting impatiently to tee up.

PUSHED HOOK:
A ball that starts to the right of the target and curves extremely back to the left.

PUSHED SLICE:
A slice which starts to the right of the target and curves farther to the right.

PUSH SHOT:
To hit the ball straight, but to the right of the intended line of flight. Not as disastrous as a slice. Also called **PUSH**.

PUSH TIED HOLES:
When three holes are tied and a player or team wins the fourth, all four holes are awarded to the winner of the fourth hole.

PUT A TACK ON IT:
A request to mark your ball.

PUTT:
Playing a stroke on the green with the putter.

PUTT OUT:
To stroke the ball into the hole.

PUSH

PUSH

PUTTER:

A straight-faced club generally used on the green. They are made in several different shapes and sizes. Also called **PUTTING CLEEK**.

PUTTING CLOCK:

Another term used for the **PRACTICE PUT-TING GREEN**.

PUTTER

PUTTING GREEN:

The ground around the hole prepared specifically for putting or otherwise defined as such by the committee. When any part of the ball touches the green, the ball is considered to be on the putting green. Also called the **PUTTING SUR-FACE, DANCE FLOOR** and **GREEN**.

PUTTING GREEN

PUTTY:

An obsolete term meaning to change the shape of the ball. Also called **ECLIPSED BALL** or **WARPED BALL**.

QUACK GRASS:
Species of grass found on a golf course.

QUACKER:
Another name for a **DUCK HOOK**.

QUADRUPLE BOGEY:
Four strokes over par.

QUAIL HIGH:
A shot hit on a low and flat trajectory.

QUALIFYING SCHOOL:
A place where aspiring professional golfers try to qualify for the PGA and LPGA Tours. Considered to be real pressure golf. Also called **Q-SCHOOL**.

QUARTER SHOT:
A shot made with a reduced swing, half of a half swing.

QUICK:
Rushing your swing or overall playing routine.

QUARTER SHOT

QUITTING:
Not hitting through the shot with conviction. Also called **DECELERATION, NEGATIVE ACCELERATION** and **QUITTING ON THE BALL**.

QUIT ON SHOT:
Failure to follow through on the shot.

R & A:
The Royal and Ancient Golf Club of St. Andrews who oversees golf in Europe, Asia and the Commonwealth.

RABBIT:
1. A beginning player. An amateur golfer with little success.
2. A topped shot that bounces erratically.
3. A touring professional who has no tournament exemptions and must compete in qualifying school for chances to play in tournaments.
4. Golf game with many variations. On the first hole, the rabbit is on the loose. The first player to win a hole is said to "hold the rabbit". The rabbit stays with his owner until another player wins a hole and the rabbit is on the loose again. A player must win a hole again to claim the rabbit. The object of the game is to have the rabbit at the end of the ninth and eighteenth holes.

RADIAL DEVIATION:
One of the possible positions of the wrists at the top of the backswing

RADIAL DEVIATION

RADIUS:
A term borrowed from geometry used to describe the distance between the center of the swing arc (the middle of the left shoulder) and the hands on the grip.

RADIUSED SOLE:
Arc or curve on the bottom of an iron club.

RAINMAKER:
A term for a very high shot.

RABBIT

RAISED SWING CENTER:
Elevating the central area in the body (somewhere between the top of the spine and center of the neck) around which rotation takes place. What the novice frequently refers to as "looking up" and which results in a swing that is too high. Also called **CHANGING THE SPINE ANGLE**.

RAKE:
1. The tool used to smooth the sand after you leave the bunker.
2. A high lofted club that is no longer in use. It was used for playing from sand and out of water.
3. To tap the ball back into the hole casually with your putter after missing the putt.

RAKE 1

RANGE:
Practice area. Also called the **DRIVING RANGE**.

RANGER:
An individual who monitors and directs play on the course.

RAP:
To hit a putt firmly, stopping the motion of the clubhead at impact.

RAP TAP:
Putt the ball with a firm stroke.

RATING MARKER:
A fixed indicator of the starting point from which the yardage rating for each hole is measured. The rating marker is located at the side of the tee.

RAP TAP

RATTLE IT IN:
When a putt bounces around the edge of the cup before dropping into the hole.

READABLE:
A putting green or aspect of a putt that can be read.

READING THE GREEN:
Assessing the path on which a putt must travel to the hole. Also called **READ**.

READY GOLF:
Name given to attempt to save time by foregoing the honor. The player ready to play first plays.

READING THE GREEN

RECOVER:
To play back into a satisfactory position on the fairway or onto the green from an undesirable position, such as a hazard.

RECOVERABILITY AND ROUGH:
The existence of heavy rough and other penalizing factors in the area around the putting surface.

RECOVERY:
Risky shots made to the fairway or putting surface from hazard areas such as the heavy rough and treed areas.

RECOVERY SHOT:
The shot played when trying to recover.

RED GRANGE:
A score made of 77, named after the number worn by the football great.

RED RANGER:
A round played in 77 stokes. Also called **SUN-SET STRIP**.

RED STAKE:
Used to indicate lateral water hazards.

REEDS:
Species of grass found on the golf course.

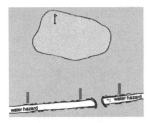

RED STAKE

REFEREE:
Anyone appointed by the committee to go along with golfers to interpret the Rules of Golf and decide questions of fact. The referee acts on any infraction of a rule he observes or that is reported to him. Referees should not handle the flagstick, mark the position of the hole, or lift or mark the position of the ball. Normally, referees are used only for competitions.

REGULAR:
A shaft with normal flex. Also called **REGULAR SHAFT**.

REGULATION:
The number of shots allowed to a hole by a scratch player.

RELAX:
1. A loosening of the hands at the top of the backswing.
2. Condition of being relaxed.
3. Give or take recreation or amusement.

RELEASE

RELEASE:
1. When the ball is hit on the green and proceeds to move forward. This type of release is the opposite of "checking up," where the ball stops quickly upon hitting the green because of the backspin.
2. The point in the downswing where the wrists unhinge. Usually just past the belt line.

RELIEF:
When you are allowed to drop a ball that was in a hazard or affected by some obstruction without penalty.

RELOAD:
To hit a second shot from the tee after losing the first.

REMEDY:
A correction or solution.

RENO PUTTS:
This golf game is a putting contest. All putts are added at the end of the round. The player with the least number of putts is the winner.

REVERSE OVERLAP:
A putting grip in which the little finger of the right hand overlaps the index finger on the left hand.

REVERSE PIVOT:
An incorrect move made during the downswing when the weight is transferred to the back foot instead of the front foot.

REVERSE OVERLAP

REVERSE WEIGHT SHIFT:
During the backswing, moving either the upper or lower part of the body in a direction opposite from that which is mechanically sound, i.e., forward (to the left) of the body's centerline rather than behind it (to the right).

RHYTHM:
A harmonious swing with a regular and repeating pattern. The tempo of your golf swing.

RIBBED:
An iron club marked with prominently scored ribs and grooves on the face; a feature now banned by the Rules of Golf.

RIFLE:
To play a shot accurately and with excellent distance.

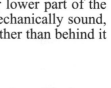

RIFLE A SHOT:
To hit the ball hard, straight and far.

RIM:
To run the ball around the edge of the cup. Also called **LIP OUT, RIMMED, TO RIM THE CUP** and **RIM OUT.**

RIM THE CUP

RIM THE CUP:
The ball touches the edge of the cup, but does not fall in. Also called **RIMMED**.

RINGER:
A golfer who usually wins. Also called a **SANDBAGGER**.

RINGER SCORE:
Your best ever score at each hole on a golf course.

RINGER TOURNAMENT:
A competition in which a competitor's lowest score made on each hole over a period of time is posted. The winner is the player with the lowest total at the end of the competition.

RINSE:
1. To sink your ball into a water hazard
2. To clean your ball with a ball washer.

ROAD HOLE:
The 17th hole at St. Andrews, one of the hardest holes in the world.

ROOSTER TAIL:
The water that is sprayed by the ball after landing on wet grass or grass that is covered in dew.

ROBBED:
When something does not go the golfer's way when he thought it should have.

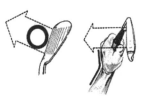

ROCK:
1. To play extremely well.
2. The ball. Also called the **PILL**.

ROLL 2

ROLL:
1. The run of a ball along the ground after landing.
2. The wrists turn over during the swing causing the ball to hook. Resulting from a rushing and forceful downswing. Also called **ROLL ON A HOLE, ROLLING, ROLL ON THE SHOT, ROLLED** and **ROLLING THE WRISTS**.
3. To play a putt so that it travels along the ground smoothly and with minimum spin.
4. Extended roll from downhill or dry ground.
5. The vertical curvature built from the crown to the sole of the face of a wood head.

ROLL IN:
To sink a putt.

ROLLER COASTER RIDE:
To play an up and down round of golf.

ROOKIE:
A former amateur during his first year of playing on the tour.

ROPE HOOK:
A low and hard hook that will run great distance after hitting the ground.

ROUGH:
Longer grass and weeded areas along the fairways, greens, or hazards. Heavier or longer grass fringing on the fairways or greens. Also called the **DEEP STUFF** and **JUNGLE**.

ROUND:

1. A complete game of golf is an 18 hole round.
2. A round of golf consists of playing nine or 18 holes.

ROUGH

ROUND ROBIN:
A tournament in which every player has the opportunity to play against every other player.

ROYAL AND ANCIENT GOLF CLUB:
The organization that runs the British Open. One of the world's oldest golf clubs, the Royal and Ancient Golf Club of St. Andrews, Scotland, had its origin as the St. Andrews Club 250 years ago. Today the organization shares responsibility with the United States Golf Association for maintaining the Rules of Golf. Also called **R&A**.

RUB OF THE GREEN:
Any accident, not caused by a player or caddie, that moves or stops a ball in play and for which no relief is given under the rules. The ball is played where it comes to rest. This is when your ball is deflected by agencies beyond your control that are not part of the match or the competitor's side in stroke play.

RUBBERCORE:
A rubber-cored ball.

RULE:
A rule as related to the game of golf may include the official Rules of Golf and any Local Rules made by the committee.

RUBBERCORE

RULES OF GOLF:

The Rules of Golf are those regulations written and interpreted by the United States Golf Association (USGA) and the Royal and Ancient Golf Club of St. Andrews, Scotland (R&A). These two organizations maintain the rules and update them at regular intervals. While using the Rules of Golf results in a uniform game regardless of the level of competition being played, the USGA and R&A can only mandate use of the rules in their own championships, such as the U.S. Open and the British Open.

RUN:

1. After the ball lands out of the air, it starts bouncing and rolling. This is the run of the ball.
2. Ball that rolls a greater distance than normal.

RUNNING IRON:

A club that is used for making short running shots.

RUN DOWN:

To hole a putt.

RUN IN:

To hole a putt.

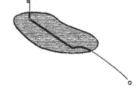

RUN UP:

To play the ball with a run-up.

RUN

RUN UP SHOT:

Used for short distances to the green where the path between the ball and the green are free from hazards.

RUT IRON:

An iron club used for playing out of ruts. Also called **RUTTER, RUTTING IRON, RUTTING NIBLICK, TRACK IRON** or **IRON NIBLICK**.

RYDER CUP:

A team match between players from the PGA European Tour and the United States PGA Tour held every four years.

RYEGRASS:

A cool season grass that dies in intense heat; similar to Poa Annua grass. Often used to overseed Bermuda grass fairways in winter to provide a heathier looking grass.

RUN UP SHOT

SAMMY:
An iron club, no longer in use, similar to the jigger but having a rounded back, used for approaching. Also referred to as the **FOUR IRON**.

SAND BAGGER:
A golfer who lies about his ability and handicap to gain an advantage.

SAND BLASTER:
A sand wedge.

SAND IRON:
1. A heavily lofted club that was used for playing from bunkers, no longer in use. It was replaced with the sand wedge.
2. A club with a broad, rounded sole and extremely lofted face, specially designed for bunkers. Also called **SAND WEDGE**.

SAND SAVE:
Anytime a player is in a trap on a hole and is still able to one-putt.

SAND TRAP:
A hazard filled with sand. A depression in the fairway, rough, or near the green; either grass or filled with sand. Also called a **BEACH, BUNKER** or **TRAP**.

SAND TEE:
A pile of sand, packed with a little water. It was used to tee the ball up on the drive. Also called **TEE**.

SAND TEE

SAND WEDGE:
An iron club used mainly for escaping from sand traps. One characteristic of the sand wedge is a heavy flange on the bottom of the club called **BOUNCE**. The bounce helps the sand wedge go through the sand easier than a pitching wedge. This club is primarily used in bunkers, but is also used on shots close to the green that require a lot of loft. Gene Sarazen invented the sand wedge by adding solder to the bottom of his pitching wedge. Also called **SAND BLASTER**.

BOUNCE

SAND WEDGE

SANDBAG:
1. To play better than your handicap indicates.
2. A golfer who plays poorly on purpose to get a high handicap to use it to his or her advantage in competition.

SANDED:
The condition of the greens when they are aerated, covered with sand and the excess sand is brushed off.

SANDING THE GREEN:
The process of placing a layer of sand and organic material on a green to smooth the surface.

SANDY (SANDIE):
Making par after being in the bunker.

SAVE:

SAVE

To recover after a misplayed shot. A well-played recovery shot.

SCARE:
The spliced joint by which wooden clubheads were fixed to shafts before the drilled socket was introduced at the end of the 19th century.

SCARED:
A wooden club having the head joined to the shaft with a scare.

SCHENECTADY PUTTER:
A center-shafted putter with an aluminum head, patented by Arthur F. Knight of Schenectady, New York, in 1903, used by Walter J. Travis in winning the British amateur championship in 1904, and shortly thereafter banned by the R. & A. Also called **SCHENECTADY**.

SCHNEIDER:
All bets are doubled if one team shuts out their opponents.

SCLAFF:
Occurs when the club hits the ground behind the ball before hitting the ball. Also called **FAT SHOT**.

SCOOP:
An improper swing in which the club has a digging or scooping action.

SCOOTER:
A topped shot that bounces sporadically.

SCLAFF

SCORECARD:
Where the score, length, par and rating of each hole is recorded.

SCORE PLAY:
Same as **STROKE PLAY.**

SCORING:
1. Colloquial term for shooting low scores.
2. The grooves on the club face.
3. Marking down the number of shots per hole or to indicate the situation of the match.

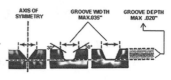

SCORING

SCORING RECORD:
A file with the most recent 20 scores posted by a player, any eligible tournament scores, USGA course rating and dates. Also called a **HANDICAP CARD**.

SCOTCH FOURSOME:
A match where the golfers alternating hitting the same ball. They also alternate driving, regardless of who holed out on the previous hole.

SCRAMBLE:
1. A game where a team of four players tees off and then picks the best shot. All then play their balls from that spot and continue throughout the round. The team with the lowest score wins.
2. To recover from missing the green or fairway and still making par or better.

SCRAMBLER:
To play erratic golf, but still score well.

SCRAPE:
An old Scottish term for a hole made by a burrowing animal. Also used to describe a slightly topped fairway or bunker shot.

SCRAPER:
An obsolete term meaning a presumably lofted wooden club.

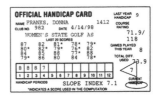

SCORING RECORD

SCRAPE IT AROUND:
To play inconsistent golf, but still post a good score.

SCRATCH:
To score equal to the par of the course. This term also refers to a player who normally shoots even par or better. A scratch player has no handicap, but a player who consistently shoots under par may have a plus handicap. For example: A scratch player, he or she plays to scratch.

SCRATCH GOLFER:
A golfer who has a zero handicap.

SCRATCH PLAY:
A golf game in which no handicaps are used.

SCUFF

SCRATCH PLAYER:
A player who does not receive any handicap strokes or has to give them up. The following additional descriptions also apply for scratch players in competitions:
  1. For men, the scratch golfer is an amateur player who plays to the standard of the field of stroke play qualifiers competing at the U.S. Amateur Championship.
  2. For women, the scratch golfer is an amateur player who plays to the standard of the match play qualifiers at the U.S. Women's Amateur Championship.

SCUFF:
  1. Hitting the ground before hitting the ball.
  2. To cut through the roots of the grass in playing the ball.

SCUFFING:
Hitting the ground behind the ball before hitting the ball. Also called **FAT, DUNCHING, CHUNKING, SCLAFFING, STUBBING** and **HEAVY.**

SCUTCH:
Species of grass found on the golf course.

SECOND BALL:
Sometimes during a tournament or match, a question arises concerning the legality of the ball in play. If the referee is unable to give a definitive ruling on the original ball, a second ball can be played and the player should hole out using both balls. After the round, the referee will make a ruling on the question. After the game, when a definitive ruling is acquired, the proper ball's score will be used for the score on the hole, i.e., the original ball in question, or the second ball if the original ball cannot be played. A second ball is not the same as a provisional ball.

SECOND CUT:
Second level of rough, higher than the first cut. Some courses have three cuts of rough.

SEDGE:
Species of grass found on the golf course.

SELECTIVE PERIMETER WEIGHTING:
Equal weight over the toe and heel of the clubhead.

SELF CONSCIOUS:
1. Being aware of one's self.
2. Made conscious of how you are appearing to others.

SEMI PRIVATE COURSE:
A course with members that is open to the public.

SEMI PRIVATE LESSON:
An instructional session which includes two to four pupils with one or more instructors.

SEMI ROUGH:
The area between the fairway and the heavy rough.

SEMI ROUGH

SENIOR:
Professional golfers are officially recognized as seniors for tournament purposes on reaching the age of 50 and for amateurs at 55.

SEPARATION:
1. When the body, arms, and legs get out of sync or position and lose the desired relationship to their contiguous parts.
2. May be the ball leaving the clubface.

SET:
A complete complement of golf clubs. The maximum number of clubs that the rules of golf allow the golfer to carry is 14. Also called **SET OF CLUBS, STICKS** and **SET MAKEUP**.

SET CONFIGURATION:
The mix of woods, irons and putters that a golfer carries at any time.

SETUP:
Your posture at address.

37°

SEVEN-IRON

SEVEN IRON:
An iron club having loft of 37-40 degrees, lie of 61-63 degrees, and length of 36 inches. Giving distance of 125-160 yards for the men and 115-150 yards for the ladies. Also called the **MASHIE-NIBLICK**.

SHAFT:
The part of the club that joins the grip to the head. The original shafts were made of hickory. Steel shafts were introduced in the 1930's and graphite shafts were introduced in the 1970's. Graphite and Titanium are also used.

SHAFT FLEX:
The measurement of the shaft's resistance to bending under any given stress.

SHAFT STIFFNESS:
The built-in degree to which a shaft will bend under a given amount of pressure.

SHAG:
To retrieve practice balls.

SHAFT

SHAG TUBE:
A golfers aid used for picking up golf balls by pressing down on the ball and it pops into the tube.

SHAG BAG:
A bag to carry practice balls.

SHAGGING:
Picking up golf balls from practice and playing areas.

SHALLOW:
1. A narrow club face. Also called **SHALLOW FACE**.
2. Flat angle of attack on the ball.

SHALLOW FACE:
Wooden headed clubs that have a face height less the normal.

SHAG TUBE

SHALLOW SWING:
Swinging the club with an upward stroke and hitting the ball on an upstroke.

SHANK:
To hit the ball with the socket or hosel of the club. Usually this causes the shot to travel sharply to the right, but it could go straight or to the left as well. Also called **SOCKETING** and **HOSELING**.

SHANK

SHAPE:
1. To move the ball deliberately from one direction to the other while in flight, purposely to hit a fade or draw. Also called **SHAPE IT**.
2. The physical condition of the golfer.

SHAPE OF SHOT:
The ball's actual line of travel, i.e., left to right, right to left or straight.

SHIFT:
The moving or shifting of the weight from one side of the body to the other.

SHOOT:
To play golf of a stated standard; make a stated score; play a hole or course in a stated score.

SHOOTING STICK:
A walking stick with a collapsible seat on top used to sit on..

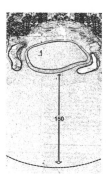

SHOOTING THE LIGHTS OUT:
To play very well.

SHORT HOLE

SHORT:
Not getting as far as the intended target. Not hitting far enough.

SHORT COURSE:
A course of less than full length, typically having mostly par three holes, some par fours, and no par fives. Also called **PAR THREE'S**.

SHORT GAME:
1. Shots played from 150 yards away from the green.
2. Approach shots to the green.

SHORT GRASS:
A shot that lands in the fairway.

SHORT HITTER:
Description of a player who does not hit the ball far.

SHORT HOLE:
Any par three hole.

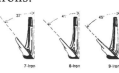

SHORT GAME

SHORT IRONS:
The highly lofted irons. The 8, 9, SW or PW irons.

SHORT STICK:
Another name for the putter. Also called the **PUTTER** and **FLAT STICK**.

SHOT:
To attempt to hit the ball or to take a stroke or swing.

SHORT IRONS

SHOTGUN START:
   A shotgun start is the term that describes when all players start at the same time but on different holes. The term stems from the gun that is fired or other sounding device used to signal when to begin play.

SHOT HOLE:
   A par three hole.

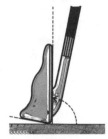

SHOT MAKER:
   A player who has the ability to play a great many different shots.

SHOT MAKING:
   The ability to play many different shots.

SHUT

SHOULDER TURN:
   The rotation of the body during the golf swing. The movement of the body or a body part around a fixed axis. Most commonly used to describe the body turning around the spine in the full backswing. Also called **PIVOT, WINDUP** and **COIL**.

SHUT:
   Clubface aligned left at address or impact, facing skyward at the top of the backswing. Also called **HOODED** or **CLOSED CLUBFACE**.

SHUT TO OPEN:
   A description of the dynamics of the clubhead when the player hoods and closes the clubface in the backswing (pointing more to the ground) then reverses it to open coming through (pointing more to the sky). Also called as **CLOSED-TO-OPEN**.

SIDE:
   1. Can mean the first nine holes (front nine) or the last nine holes (back nine) of the course.
   2. Two or more players who are partners.

SIDEHILL LIE:
   A lie with the ball either above or below your feet.

SIDESADDLE

SIDESADDLE:
   A putting style where the player faces the hole while taking his stroke. This is illegal. Also called **CROQUET STYLE**.

SINGLE:
   1. Term that is used to describe one golfer.
   2. One player against another.

SINK:
   To make a putt.

SINKER:
   1. An obsolete term meaning a golf ball that would sink in water.
   2. A well-holed putt.

SIT:
   A term used to encourage the ball to stop rolling.

SITTER:
   A ball sitting on top of the grass in the rough.

SIX-IRON

SIX IRON:
   An iron club having loft of 33-36 degrees, loft of 60-61 degrees, and length of 36 1/2 inches. Giving distance of 135-180 yards for the men and 125-165 yards for the ladies. Also called **SPADE** or **SPADE-MASHIE**.

SKINS:
   A betting game where the lowest score on the hole wins the pot. If the hole is tied, the money carries over to the next hole. Also called **SYNDICATES, CATS AND SCATS** and **SCATS**.

SKULL:
   When the leading edge of the club strikes the ball above the center rather then the clubface.

SKULL

SKULLING:
   A swinging error, generally refers to a pitch or chip shot that is hit above the center of the ball. Hitting the ball at or above its center causing the ball to be hit too hard and travel too great a distance.

SKY:
   Hitting a ball much higher than normal.

SKYING:
   A ball that flies off the top of the clubface very high and short.

SKYING

SKYWRITTING:
   A swinging error in which the clubhead makes a loop or circle at the top of the backswing. Usually causes the ball to be shanked.

SLAM DUNK:
   A putt that is hit at a fast rate of speed, hitting the back of the cup and dropping in.

SLEEVE OF BALLS:
 Box of three balls.

SLICE:
 A ball hit with a sharp curve to the right of the
 intended line of flight.

SLICER:
 One who habitually slices the ball.

SLEEVE OF BALLS

SLICING SPIN:
 It is the rotation put on the ball that spins the ball from the outside-in
 causing the ball to fly to the right.

SLICK:
 Term used to describe a fast putting surface.

SLIDER:
 1. A low hit shot that takes erratic bounces.
 2. A putt that breaks slightly in either direction.
 3. A low and hard left-to-right shot.

SLOPE:
 Adjusts your handicap to the difficulty of the
 course you play. The more difficult the course,
 the more strokes you need.

SLICE

SLOPE RATING:
 The USGA's mark that indicates the measurement of the relative difficulty of a course for players who are not scratch golfers compared to
 the course rating.

SLUMP:
 A prolonged period of bad play.

SMILE:
 A cut or gauge in the ball caused by the clubhead. Also called **CRACK**
 and **CUT**.

SMOKED:
 A ball that is hit hard and for a long distance.

SMOTHER:
 To hit the ball with a closed clubface; results
 in a low hooking shot.

SMOTHER

SMOTHERED HOOK:
A hook that drives quickly to the ground, usually directly to the left, but may start to the right. Caused by an exaggerated closed clubface.

SNAKE:
A long putt with plenty of break that rolls into the cup. Also called **FIELD GOAL.**

SNAP HOOK:
Severe hook.

SOLE

SNIPE:
A sharply hooked ball that dives quickly.

SNIPER:
A golfer who hits hooks consistently.

SNOWMAN:
Scoring an eight on a hole.

SOLE:
SOLE PLATE
1. The bottom of the club.
2. Setting the bottom of the club down on the ground at address. Also called **SOLING THE CLUB** and **SOLING.**

SOLE PLATE:
A piece of metal attached to the bottom of a wooden club.

SOLE WEIGHTING:
The distribution of weight on a wood or iron head as low in the head as it can be placed. Encourages a higher trajectory shot.

SOLHEIM CUP:
A competition between the female professional golfers of the United States and Britain held every four years.

SPADE MASHIE:
A deep-faced iron club, no longer in use, somewhat more lofted than a mashie. Also called **SIX IRON** or **SPADE.**

SPEED OF PLAY:
The pace at which a round of golf is played; the time it takes to complete a round. Ideally, a round of golf should take no more than 4 hours to play. Unfortunately, on today's crowded public courses, rounds can take as long as 5-1/2 hours to play.

SPGA:
Senior Professional Golf Association.

SPIKE MARK:
Marks on the green made by golf shoes. Also called **CLEAT MARK**.

SPIKE WRENCH:
The instrument used to attach, tighten, or remove cleats from the bottom of golf shoes.

SPINACH:
The high and heavy rough.

SPINE ANGLE:
The angle that the spine is set at address.

SPIKE WRENCH

SPINOUT:
Knees moving too fast in relation to the upper body on the downswing. Legs moving too fast in relation to the upper body on the downswing.

SPLASH SHOT:
1. A shot played from a good lie in a sand bunker in which the club bounces or splashes through the sand, cutting it from beneath the ball.
2. A shot played from a water hazard.

SPLIT HANDED GRIP:
Putting method with the hands apart to grip the club.

SPONGER:
Portable golf ball cleaner.

SPLIT HANDED
GRIP

SPOON:
A wooden head club with considerable loft and a shaft shorter than a **DRIVER** and **BRASSIE**. Also called the **THREE WOOD**.

SPOT:
To mark the position of a ball on the green before lifting it by placing a coin or small object at the back-side of the ball.

SPOT PUTTING:
Aiming for a point on the green in which the ball must roll over if it is going to fall into the cup.

SPONGER

SPRAY SHOTS:
To hit the ball erratically off line. Also called **SPRAYING**.

SPREAD EAGLE:
To utterly defeat a field of golfers in stroke play.

SPRING:
The flex of the shaft.

SPURGE:
A species of grass found on the golf course.

SQUARE

SQUARE:
1. The score of the match is even. Or the clubface and stance are aligned perfectly with the target.
2. When the clubface is placed at right angles to the imaginary ball-to-target line.
3. To the stance when a line drawn across the heels is parallel to the target line; to the shoulders, hips, and knees in aiming when they are also parallel to the tar get line.
4. To center-faced contact with the ball when it is struck. When the club is at 90 degrees to the tangent of the arc, anywhere on that arc.

SQUARE

SQUARE FACE:
When the clubface is looking directly at the hole at address and impact.

SQUARE GROOVES:
USGA banned the used of them on clubfaces.

SQUARELY:
The act of aligning oneself parallel to the target line and the bottom edge of the club perpendicular to the target.

ST. ANDREWS:
A golf course located in Fife, Scotland.

STAB:
A half hearted swing, or one lacking the proper arc.

SQUARE

STABLEFORD:

In this form of stroke competition, golfers play against a fixed score at each hole. Players receive one point for a par, two points for a birdie, five for an eagle, and ten for an albatross. Conversely, a player would receive no points for a bogey, minus one point for a double bogey and minus three for a triple bogey. The competitor scoring the highest number of points wins.

STAKE IT:

To hit the ball close to the hole. Also called **STONEY**.

STAKED TREE:

Any tree or shrub tied to a stake. If the ball is unplayable because the staked tree is interfering with the game, the player is allowed a free drop.

STANCE:

The position of the feet, hands, weight, and ball at address.

STAND ON IT:

When a golfer swings their best and gets the maximum distance out of the club.

STAKED TREE

STAND PLEASE:

The shout used to request spectators to remain motionless and silent while a player is shooting.

STANDARD SCRATCH SCORE (SSS):

1. The assessment of par for a course and the basis for handicapping.
2. The total number of shots that would be expected to complete 18 holes of the course under normal conditions. Playing off a handicap of zero, or scratch. Some allowance may be given for the ease or difficulty of the hole. The round would be played off the competition tees from which the course had been officially measured.

STARTER:

One who controls when groups tee off, usually on the first tee.

STARTING TIME:

The time you tee off from the first tee.

STEAL:

An obsolete term meaning long improbable putt that just holes out.

STEER:
> An exaggerated attempt to control the shot which results in losing the desired distance and/or direction.

STICK:
> 1. The flagstick.
> 2. A ball landing out of the air and stopping immediately with very little roll.
> 3. A ball landing out of the air and imbedding itself in the ground.

STICKS:
> Another name for your set of golf clubs.

STIFF:
> 1. A shaft with reduced flex.
> 2. A shot hit close to the cup.

STIFF ONE:
> To hit an approach shot close to the pin.

STOBBIE

STIMPMETER:
> A device used to measure the speed of the greens. This speed is based upon the distance the ball rolls once it is released from the meter. Stimpmeter reading in the 5 to 6 range means slow greens, 7 to 8 means medium, 9 to 10 mean fast and 11 and over means extremely fast according to the PGA Tournament speeds.

STINKWEED:
> Species of grass found on the golf course.

STIPULATED ROUND:
> Playing the holes of a course in their correct sequence. A stipulated round usually consists of 18 holes, unless otherwise authorized by the committee. The stipulated round can be extended by the committee to settle a tie in either match play or stroke play by as many holes as are needed for someone to win the match.

STOBBIE:
> An approach shot to the green which lands by the flagstick within the length of the putter head.

STONY:
> To hit a ball close to the flagstick. Also called **STIFF, STAKE IT** and **HITTING STIFF.**

STOP:
Backspin, causing a pitched ball to stop dead or nearly so on impact.

STOP THE BLEEDING:
1. To make a par or better after bogeying several holes prior.
2. This phrase means to stop losing points, strokes or money.

STORE SET:
A golf club set that is purchased in a store. Usually including the 1, 3, and 5 woods and 3, 4, 5, 6, 7, 8, 9, PW. The putter is not included in most **STORE SETS**. Also called **STORE BOUGHT**.

STRAIGHTAWAY:
A hole having a straight fairway.

STRAIGHT FACED:
1. Refers to a club with little or no loft on the face.
2. An iron club with little or no loft on the face, or a wood without normal budge and roll.

STRAIGHT FLIGHT:
Any ball traveling in a straight line while in flight is said to be in straight flight.

STRAIGHT HITTER:
Golfer who hits the ball consistently straight.

STRIKE OFF:
To drive from the tee.

STRIPED IT:
A tee shot that is hit well.

STRAIGHTAWAY

STROKE:
Any forward movement of the club with the intention of hitting the ball. It counts as one stroke, even if you miss the ball, because your intention was to hit the ball.

STROKE AND DISTANCE:
The penalty of one stroke and the return to the site of the shot before, when a ball is unplayable.

STROKE COUNTERS:
Instruments used to keep track of your score.

STROKE HOLE:

A stroke hole is one on which a golfer applies a handicap stroke. The order in which handicap strokes are designated appears on the scorecard. The toughest hole on a course is called the "number one stroke hole." The easiest hole is the "number 18 stroke hole."

STROKE INDEX:

1. All holes are graded according to their difficulty. The hardest is stroke index 1.The easiest is stroke index 10.
2. The numbers on a scorecard indicating the order of the holes in which a handicap golfer receives his strokes.

STROKE LOFT:

Less loft than normal for any given club. Generally encourages more distance.

STROKE PLAY:

Golf game decided by the number of strokes taken. Competition by the total overall score. The one with the lowest score is the winner.

STROKE SAVERS:

Accurate shooting near the green.

STROKEMAKER:

A shot maker.

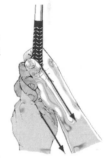

STRONG GRIP

STROKES AS THEY FALL:

The strokes are the handicap strokes a player is entitled to in a match. They are applied to a player's score on a hole-by-hole basis to determine a player's net score for each hole starting with the hardest hole and moving down to the easiest.

STRONG GRIP:

Grip whereby the left-hand is rolled on top of the golf club, the right hand is rolled underneath the golf grip (for the right-handed golfer). An exaggerated clockwise rotational positioning of the hands when placed on the grip, i.e., left hand more on top of the shaft, right-hand more under. Also called **CLOSED-FACE GRIP**.

STUB:

A short shot, usually a chip, that you hit fat or stick the club in the ground.

STUBBING:
 A shot in which the clubhead strikes the ground before striking the ball, causing a partial hit, decreasing the distance the ball travels Also called **DUNCHING, SCUFFING, CHUNKING, SCLAFFING, HEAVY** and **FAT**.

STYLIST:
 A golfer whose swing is admired as correct, consistent, and esthectically pleasing.

STYMIE:
 1. A ball obstructing your line to the hole - now obsolete because the ball is lifted and marked.
 2. A player blocked with an obstacle such as a tree.
 3. Golf game played on the green.
 4. Scotch meaning, "the faintest form of anything."

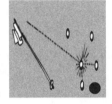

STYMIE

SUCK BACK:
 A ball that hits the green and then reverses direction due to back-spin.

SUCKER PIN:
 A flag placed close to a hazard.

SUDDEN DEATH PLAY OFF:
 If there is a tie, the competition is decided by a sudden death playoff. The person to win a hole is deemed the winner.

SUMMER RULES:
 In summer rules, the ball is played as it lies and the lie cannot be changed or improved. Summer rules are the standard rules, as opposed to winter rules, which are usually local. Also called **SUMMER GOLF**.

SUNDAY BAG:
 A bag designed to carry fewer clubs than larger bags.

SUNSET STRIP:
 A round played in 77 strokes. Also called **RED RANGER**.

SUPERINTENDENT:
 A person responsible for the upkeep of the course.

SUNDAY BAG

SUPINATE:
 To rotate the wrist so that the palm of the hand faces upward.

SUPINATION:
The rotation of the wrist so that the palm of the hand faces upward. In the golf swing, it is the right-hand rotation motion on the backswing and the left hand's on the forward swing.

SURLYN:
A material from which most balls are made.

SURLYN BALL:
Solid center, harder cover, more durable ball, appropriate for the majority of golfers.

SUSPENSION RADIUS:
The distance from a point at the base of the neck to the ball that is used as a reference to determine the spine angle inclination and whether or not the swing center has moved.

SWALE:
A depression or dip in the terrain.

SWAY:
To move to the right excessively on the backswing.

SWEEPING MOTION

SWEEPING MOTION:
The act of swinging where the club is low on the backswing and low on the downswing, creating a broom like or sweeping motion. Opposite of chopping down and steep angle.

SWEET SPOT:
The perfect point on the clubface with which to strike the ball.

SWEET SPOT

SWING:
The swing is the continuous movement of the clubhead.

SWING ARC:
The entire path the clubhead follows in its complete motion away from and toward the target. It has the dimensions of both length and width. Also called **SWING PLANE, PLANE** and **ARC**.

SWING CENTER:
A point around which the roughly circular motion of the swinging of the arms and upper trunk are made. It is located between the base of the neck and top of the spine. Not necessarily fixed, it remains generally constant in the small swings, with some movement allowed as the swing gets longer. Nevertheless, if the movement of the swing center is too great, the overall timing of the swing becomes more difficult. Also called **HUB**.

SWING DOCTOR:
A teaching professional.

SWING DONUT:
A donut shaped weight that is use to make the club heavier when swung during warm up or practice. Also called **SWING WEIGHT**.

SWING PATHS:
1. In-to-in   (Inside to Inside)
2. In-to-Out   (Inside to Out)
3. Out-to-in   (Outside to In)

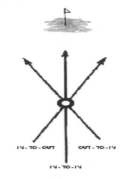

SWING PATHS

SWING PATTERN:
1. Posture at Address
2. Backswing
3. Top of backswing
4. Downswing
5. Follow-through

SWING PLACE:
An imaginary, flat, thin surface which is used to describe the path and angle on which the club is swung. Plane has inclination or tilt, i.e., flat, medium, upright, as well as direction inside, down the line, or outside.

SWING SPEED:
The speed of the clubhead throughout impact.

SWING THOUGHT:
An easy to remember aid to hitting the ball.

SWING WEIGHT

SWING WEIGHT:
1. The lorythmic scale is used to measure the swing weight.
2. A measurement that indicates the distribution of weight in a golf club from grip to clubhead.
3. Letter and number combination expressing the measurement of swing weight. They are as follows; C0 - C5, C6 - C8, C9 - D2 and D3 - D5.
4. The measurement of balance and overall weight of the clubs in a matched set. All clubs should feel the same when swung.
5. A donut shaped weight that is use to make the club heavier when swung during warm up or practice. Also called **SWING DONUT**.

SWINGER:
A player using a style of striking the ball which primarily employs body rotation, firm grip pressure and good rhythm to maximize centrifugal force.

SWING DONUT

SWINGING TYPES:
1. Length of Backswing - Short or long backswing.
2. Speed of Swing - The speed of the backswing and downswing.
3. Swinging Plane - A flat or upswing plane. Flat swing moves horizontally rather then in an upright plane.

SWIPE:
An obsolete term meaning to play a full and powerful shot from the tee.

SYNDICATES:
A betting game where the lowest score on the hole wins the pot. If the hole is tied, the money carries over to the next hole. Also called **SKINS, SCATS** and **CATS AND SKATS**.

TAGGED IT:
Refers to a shot hit a long way.

TAILWIND:
A breeze that blows in the same direction as the shot, helping the ball fly further. A wind blowing from behind the golfer toward the target. Also called **BACKWIND** and **DOWNWIND**.

TAKE AWAY:
When you begin to bring back the clubhead on the back swing. This movement should be done low and deliberate.

TAKE IT DEEP:
To shoot a very low score.

TAKE OVER:
To take a second shot from the tee after losing the first shot. Also called **MULLIGAN**.

TAKE THE PIPE:
Collapsing under pressure at a critical stage of competition.

TALK TO IT:
Golfers who talk to the ball.

TAP IN:
1. A very short putt.
2. To make a very short putt.

TARGET:
Where the golfer intends the ball to land.

TAKE AWAY

TARGET LINE:
An imaginary line which runs from the ball to the intended target.

TARGET SIDE:
The side of the body or ball that is closest to the hole or target where the golfer is aiming.

TEE:
1. A wooden or plastic peg used for setting the ball up off of the grass. Originally a pile of sand was used to elevate the ball for driving. Also called **PEG** and **TEE PEG**.
2. The area where the golfer begins the hole. Also called **TEE BOX** and **TEEING GROUND**.

TEED:
1. A ball at rest between the tee and the green lying supported and accessible. Also called **TEED UP, SITTING PREETY** and **GOOD LIE**.
2. A ball that has placed on a peg or tee.

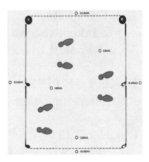

TEE

TEEING GROUND:
The teeing ground is the starting place for each hole -- a rectangular area two club-lengths deep, with the outside limits of two tee markers defining the front and sides of the area. You can tee your ball anywhere in that rectangle, but you are not required to stand within it. A ball must be positioned completely outside of this rectangular area for it to be considered outside of the teeing ground.

TEE BOX:
The starting place for the hole to be played. Usually indicated by two markers. Also called the **TEE GROUND** and **TEE**.

TEE MARKER:
An object that determines the minimum distance a golfer must stand from the hole when he or she drives. Also called a **MARKER** and **TEES**.

TEE OFF:
To play a tee shot. Also called **TEE SHOT**.

TEE BOX

TEE PEG:
You can put the ball on this device for your first shot to help raise the ball off the ground. It is then much easier to attain height. Also called **TEE** and **PEG**.

TEE SHOT:
A shot played from the tee. Also called **TEE OFF**.

TEE TIME:
A tee time is a specific time designated for a golfer to begin his or her round.

TEE UP:
To begin playing by placing the ball on the tee.

TEE UP

TEMPER:
State of mind; disposition or mood.

TEMPO:
The rhythm of your swing. The pace or speed a golfer desires to swing when he or she attempts to strike the ball.

TEMPORARY GREEN:
Used in the winter to preserve the permanent green.

TENDING THE FLAG:
To tend the flag is to stand by the flag while another member of the group is putting. This usually occurs on the longer putts. Once the ball is on its way toward the hole, the person tending the flag should take the flag out of the hole so the flagstick does not interfere with the putt. Also called **ATTENDING THE FLAG**.

TENSION:
1. A stretching of mind or body.
2. A strained condition.
3. Mental or nervous strain.
4. Stress cause by a pulling force.

TENDING THE FLAG

TESTER PUTT:
A putt that is long enough not to be a **GIMME** and short enough for an average player to hole. Also called a **YIPS PUTT** and **TESTER**.

TEXAS SCRAMBLE:
Golf game that is a variation of the **SCRAMBLE**.

TEXAS WEDGE:
A shot played on the fringe or fairway with the putter. What a putter is called when it is used off the green.

THAT DOG WILL HUNT:
Expression used by a golfer who just hit a good shot.

THAT OLD DOG JUST WON'T HUNT:
Expression used by golfers when they hit a shot that is unplayable.

THAT'LL PLAY:
Refers to a good or mediocre shot.

TEXAS WEDGE

THAT'S GOOD:
1. A good hit or lie
2. Expression used when conceding a putt.

THIN:
Hitting the ball with the clubhead traveling on too high a line, catching the ball above center.

THIN

THIN SHOT:
A thin shot is one in which the golfer hits the ball above its center, causing the ball to skip or roll along the ground rather than rise into the air. Also called **TOPPING** or **BLADED**.

THIRD:
An expression used in handicapping, meaning that one of the players is allowed a stroke on one-third of the hole or six strokes on 18 holes.

THREAD:
To direct the ball through a narrow opening.

THREESOME:
1. A group consisting of three golfers.
2. A best-ball match between one player and two playing as partners. Also called **THREE BALL MATCH**.

THREE BALL MATCH:
1. A match in which three players play one ball each, and each is playing a match against each of the other two.
2. A best-ball match between one player and two playing as partners. Also called **THREESOME**.

THREE IRON:
An iron club having loft of 23-25 degrees, lie of 57-59 degrees, and length of 38 inches. Giving distance of 165-210 yards for the men and 145-185 yards for the ladies. Also called **MID-MASHIE**.

THREE JACK:
To three putt a hole. Also called **THREE PUTT** and **SNAKIE**.

THREE IRON

THREE OFF THE TEE:
If a ball is lost, out of bounds, or unplayable from the tee shot, the player is penalized one stroke and tees off again making it their third shot. Refers to **MULLIGAN**.

THREE OVER:
Three over par.

THREE PUTT:
Undesirable number of putts taken on a green. Also called **THREE JACK** and **SNAKIE**.

THREE QUARTER SHOT

THREE QUARTER SHOT:
Less than a full swing. A shot made with a reduced swing.

THREE WOOD:
A wood club having loft of 15-17 degrees, lie of 55-57 degrees, and length of 42 inches. Giving distance of 200-250 yards for the men and 175-225 yards for the ladies. Also called the **SPOON**.

THROUGH SWING:
The part of the swing during which the ball is actually hit. Also called impact.

THROUGH THE GREEN:
All areas of the course, except the teeing ground and putting green of the hole being played or any hazards on the course.

TIGER:
A player having a good scoring streak.

TIGER COUNTRY:
The heavy rough.

THREE WOOD

TIGER TEE:
The teeing ground located the farthest distance from the hole, used by the better players. Also called **BACK TEE** and **CHAMPIONSHIP TEE**.

TIGHT:
1. A fairway that is narrow or having narrow fairways.
2. A lie sitting down close to the ground.

TIGHT FAIRWAY:
A narrow fairway.

TIGHT LIE:
A ball on bare ground.

TIMING:
The pace and sequence of the movement during the swing.

TIP:
A suggestion that may or may not improve your game.

TIGHT FAIRWAY

TIPPED SHAFT:
A shaft in which a small portion of the tip, or clubhead end of the shaft, is cut off. This is an advanced technique practiced by the professionals. Tipping produces a stiffer feel of the club.

TITANIUM:
Metal used in lightweight shafts.

TOE:
Forward part of the clubhead.

TOED

TOED:
A shot hit too far toward the toe of the club. Also called **TOE JOB**, **TOED SHOT** or **TOE IN**.

TOE IN:
A clubhead having a specially prominent toe with a slightly turned-in face.

TOE JOB:
A shot hit too far towards the toe of the club. Also called **TOED**, **TOED SHOT** or **TOE IN**.

TOP:
Striking the ball above its equator causing the ball to skip or roll along the ground rather than rise into the air. A golfer who hits a ball in this manner is said to "blade one." Also called **BLADING** and **TOPPING**.

TOPOGRAPHY:
1. The lay out and mapping of the land on a golf course or hole.
2. Elevation change around and on the green.
3. The difficulty in taking your stance when addressing the ball.

TOPPED THE BALL:
Striking only the top half of the ball with the club, rather than striking the bottom half. The result is a shot that will roll just a few feet before stopping. It is definitely a mis-hit.

TOPPING:
When taking your swing, you hit the top portion of the ball instead of hitting the center of the ball.

TOP LINE:
The top of an iron head where the face and back meet.

TOPPING

TOP OF THE BACKSWING:
The area at the end of your backswing before you begin your down swing.

TOP SPIN:
The forward rotation of the ball in motion.

TORQUE:
1. A twisting of the shaft at impact.
2. The amount of rotating twist that occurs in a golf shaft during the swing.

TOP OF BACKSWING

TORSION:
A degree of twist occurring in the shaft of the club during the golf swing.

TOSSING BALLS:
A way to decide who will be partners during a match. One golfer takes a ball from each player and tosses them all into the air together. Whoever owns the two balls coming to rest closest to each other are partners.

TOUCH:
Accuracy and aptitude, especially in approaching and putting.

TOUCH AND FEEL:
The ability to judge distances accurately and putt with delicacy.

TOUCH SHOT:
A very delicately hit shot.

TOUR:
A series of tournaments for a professional.

TOURING PRO:
A professional tournament player, as opposed to a teaching or club PGA pro.

TOURNAMENT:
A tournament is an organized competition in either stroke or match play. When both professional and amateur golfers participate, the competition is described as an "open."

TOURNAMENT SCORE:
A score made in a competition with the winner decided in accordance with Stipulated Rounds and the Rules of Golf. A committee oversees the competition and decides whether or not the score can be identified by the letter "T." Certain inter-club competition scores could be recorded as tournament scores. They are team matches; competitions restricted by age; member-guest competitions; rounds qualifying individuals for competition on the city, state, and national level; and competitions held by golf associations. INTRA-CLUB competition scores such as low gross-low net competitions; fourball match or stroke-play competitions; and club championships which are stroke or match play, scratch or with handicap should be recorded as tournament scores when they meet the above conditions.

TRACK:
The golf course. Also called **GOLF COURSE, GREEN** and **COURSE**.

TRACK IRON:
An obsolete club that was used primarily to hit the ball from cart tracks. A club used in the early days of golf with a small round head. Also called **RUT IRON** or **NIBLICK**.

TRACKING:
A putt hit on a perfect line to the hole.

TRACKING HANDICAP INDEX:
The handicap index represents the golfing skill of a player on a course of standard difficulty. The Tracking Handicap Index is determined by the handicap parameters you choose. For example, if you choose the USGA Handicap Parameters your Tracking Handicap Index is computed the same as a USGA Handicap Index.

TRADESMEN ENTRANCE:
The ball rolling in the cup from the rear on a sloped green.

TRAJECTORY:
The flight of the ball. The height and flight pattern of the ball after it has been hit.

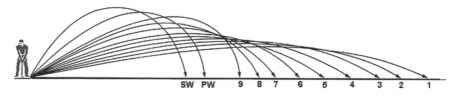

TRAJECTORY

TRANSITION:
The change of direction in the swing from back to forward, from away to toward.

TRAP:
A hazard filled with sand. A depression in the fairway, rough, or near the green, either grass or filled with sand. Also called a **BEACH, SAND TRAP** or **BUNKER**

TREES:
Referring to the difficulty of the course. The strategic location, size, height, and density of the trees.

TREND HANDICAP:
An unofficial estimate of a handicap, which may include scores. The **TREND HANDICAP** can not be used for formal competitions.

TRIPLE BOGEY:
Three shots over par.

TROLLEY:
Cart used for carrying the clubs. Also called a **GOLF CART, PULL CART** and **CART**.

TROUBLE:
Rough, hazards, trees, or other obstacles on the course.

TROUBLE SHOT:
A shot taken from a bad lie such as from behind trees or in the rough.

TROUBLE WOOD:
1. Any wood used out of the rough or hazard.
2. Any wood with a greater loft than the **FIVE WOOD**. The most common club used is the **SEVEN WOOD**.

TURF:
Soil bound together by grass to form a thick mat.

TURN:
1. Making your way to the back nine holes.
2. The rotation of the upper body during the swing. Also called **COIL**.

TURN IT OVER:
To hit a draw. To hit the ball from right to left.

TWITCH:
1. A nervous reaction to a situation.
2. Putting nerves or to mis-hit a putt from an attack of the twitch.

TWO IRON:
An iron club having loft of 19-22 degrees, lie of 57-59 degrees, and length of 38 1/2 inches. Giving distance of 175-210 yards for the men and 165-195 yards for the ladies. Also called the **MID-IRON** and **CLEEK**.

TWO PUTT:
To hole the ball in two putting strokes.

TWO SHOT:
A hole requiring a drive and another full shot to reach the green.

TWO-IRON

TWO SHOTTER:
A two-shot hole.

TWOSOME:

1. A pair of golfers playing together in a stroke competition.
2. A group consisting of two golfers.

TWO WOOD:

A wood club having loft of 13-14 degrees, lie of 54-56 degrees, and length of 42-1/2 inches. Giving distance of 220-270 yards for the men and 185 -225 yards for the ladies. Also called a **BRASSIE**.

TWO WOOD

U.S. OPEN:
National men's golf championship of America.

U.S. WOMEN'S OPEN:
National women's golf championship of America.

UGLY:
1. A bad shot.
2. Anything bad that happens to you on the course.
3. Expression used instead of swearing. "Man that was **UGLY**".

UMBRELLA:
A light, portable, circular cover for protection against rain or sun, consisting of fabric held on a folding frame.

UNACCEPTABLE SCORE:
Several factors make a score unacceptable for handicap purposes. Scores earned under the following circumstances may not be part of a golfer's scoring record:
1. A player's score may be unacceptable if he/she is using clubs that do not meet the standards set by the USGA.
2. The round is played in an area in which an inactive season has been established by the golf association in control.
3. Fewer than 13 holes are played. An exception to this condition allows consecutive nine-hole scores to be used.
4. Most of the holes on a course are not played according to the Rules of Golf.
5. The length of the 18-hole golf course is under 3,000 yards.

UMBRELLA

UNCOCK:
The unhinging of the wrists at the belt line resulting in the whip on the shot. Also called **UNHINGE**.

UNDER CLUB:
To use one club less than what is needed for the shot.

UNDER CLUBBING:
Not taking a full swing with the club you are using.

UNDER PAR:
Scoring fewer strokes than the par figure for a hole, a round of 18 holes, or a tournament. For example, "She was one under par on that hole. He was four under par for the round. She was 12 under par for the tournament."

UNDER SPIN:
Same as backspin.

UNDULATING GREEN:
A green with a lot of slopes, waves and bends to the surface.

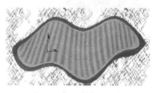

UNDULATING GREEN

UNLAP:
All ten fingers are in contact with the grip of the club. Also called the **BASEBALL GRIP** and **TEN FINGER GRIP**.

UNPLAYABLE LIE:
You cannot hit the ball from the position it is in. Usually awarded with a one stroke penalty.

UP:
1. Ahead in the match.
2. The person next to play.
3. Coming close to the hole with a putt or approach.
4. A shot reaching the green.

UP AND DOWN:
1. This term applies to the holes on which a golfer reaches the green with a greater than regulation number of strokes, but is able to one-putt the hole.
2. Getting out of trouble or a hazard and into the hole.
3. Getting onto the green and putting out.
4. When the level of play alternates between good and bad.

UP AND OUT:
To get the ball into the hole in two strokes from just off the green or on the edge of the green. Like chipping in for two.

UPHILL LIE:
When the ball is located on an uphill slope with the grade descending away from the target.

UPRIGHT:
When the lie angle is more vertical or erect than normal.

UNLAP

UPRIGHT STANCE:
Improper stance in which the player is standing too erect up to the ball. Usually caused by improper knee bend.

UPRIGHT SWING:
A swing with a steep plane. The club movement is almost vertical.

UPSHOT:
To hit a high shot short of the target. Also called **UPSHOOT**.

UPWIND:
When the wind blows at your face when you are looking at the green. Also called **HEADWIND**.

UPWIND

USGA:
United States Golf Association. The USGA , founded in 1894, is the ruling body for golf in the United States. The USGA, along with the Royal and Ancient Golf Club of St. Andrews, Scotland, wrote the Rules of Golf. Every four years, the rules are updated as deemed appropriate.

USGA COURSE RATING:
The playing difficulty of a course with regard to the ability of a scratch golfer under normal course and weather conditions.

USGA HANDICAP INDEX:
A number that indicates the ability of a golfer on a course of average difficulty.

USGA HANDICAP SYSTEM:
A method of evaluating golf skills so that golfers of different abilities can compete on an equitable basis.

USGA SLOPE RATING:
The slope rating determines the playing difficulty for the players who are not scratch golfers.

UTILITY WOOD:
A wood designed for playing from bad lies and from the rough. Usually a higher lofted clubhead with a longer shaft than normal. Sometimes features rails or ridges on the sole to aid in the digging action on bad lies. Often made in the form of the 5, 7, or 9 woods.

U-TURN:
A putt that rolls all the way around the edge of the cup before coming out. Also called **HORSESHOE**.

V'S:
The V's formed by the thumb and forefinger of each hand when gripping the club.

VALLEYS:
1. The flat areas between mounds on an undulating green.
2. When a golfer is in a slump.

VALLEY OF DEATH:
Famous hollow in front of the 18th green on the old course at St. Andrews, Scotland. Also called **VALLEY OF SIN**.

VAMPIRE:
A spin that makes the ball tend to stop rather than roll when it lands. Also called **OVERBITE, BITE, BICUSPID** or **BACKSPIN**.

VARDON GRIP:
A type of **OVERLAPPING GRIP**.

VECTOR:
A quantity or measure related to force that has both magnitude and direction. An important factor in determining the distance and direction a ball travels.

VARDON GRIP

VELOCITY:
The velocity rule with the manufacturers of golf balls is with a limit of 250 feet (76.2 meters) per second.

VEGAS SHOOT OUT:
This golf game is played in foursomes. The combined scores of each team determines the teams score.

VICTORY LAP:
When a putt circles around the rim of the cup before falling into the hole.

VIPER GRASS:
Species of grass found on the golf course.

VISUALIZATION

VISUALIZATION:
Using the mind to picture the shot you play before its execution.

WAGGLE:
The preliminary movement taken to get the body in motion just before you swing.

WAGON:
Another name for a **GOLF CART**.

WALK IN BET:
A bet made with someone that is not playing in your foursome or group.

WALKER CUP:
An amateur team match between Britain, Ireland, and the United States.

WARM UP:
Practice or exercise for a few minutes before playing a round of golf.

WATER BALL:
1. A golf ball intended for shots over water. Also called **POND BALL**.
2. Beat up balls that are intended to be used to shoot over water. Also called **POND BALL**.
3. Ball shot into the water. Also called **POND BALL** and **DEPTH CHARGE**.
4. A specially made ball that does not sink but floats in the water.

WATER CLUB:
This club is now obsolete. It was used from the 1880's to the 1930's and was designed for playing the ball from water hazards.

WATER HAZARD:
Any ocean, sea, lake, river, pond, ditch, drain ditch, stream, or any other water way.

WATER HOLE:
When a pond or stream is positioned so that a golfer must shoot over the water in order to play the hole, the hole is referred to as a water hole.

WATERY GRAVE

WATERY GRAVE:
Balls shot into a water hazard. Also called **WATER BALL, POND BALL** and **DEPTH CHARGE**.

WEAK GRIP:
The currently used expression to describe an exaggerated, counterclockwise, toward-the-left shoulder rotational positioning of the hands when placed on the club. Changed to Open-Face Grip. This is more descriptive, does not imply an over-relaxed hold, and, in its application, is parallel to other golf terms such as "open stance."

WEAK LOFT:
More loft than normal for any given club. Encourages less distance on the shot.

WEAK GRIP

WEDGE:
An iron club used primarily for playing pitches to the green, having loft of 50-52 degrees, lie of 63-65 degrees, and length of about 35 inches, and having a flange less prominent than that of the sand wedge behind and below the leading edge, to prevent the clubhead from digging into grass. Giving distances of 85-140 yards for the men and 75-125 yards for the ladies. Used to hit a pitch shot. Also called **WEDGE**.

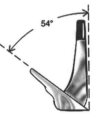

WEIGHT DISTRIBUTION:
The percentage of weight placed on either foot at address.

WEIGHT SHIFT:
Body weight transferred from one side to the other.

WEDGE

WHIFF:
To miss the ball completely. Also called **AIR BALL, AIR SHOT, FAN, SILENT** and **NO NOISE BALL**.

WHINS:
A British term for the rough or brush. Also called **GORSE BUSH**.

WHIP:
The unhinging of the hands and sweeping the clubhead throughout the hitting area. One of the major sources of power.

WHIPPED IT AROUND:
A term used when you have played well.

WHIP

WHIPPING:
1. To whip the clubhead throughout the hitting area.
2. The string wrapping around the neck of a wood club. Prevents cracking from repeated impact.

WHIPPY:
A shaft with more flex than normal.

WHITE STAKES:
Used as the out-of-bounds marker.

WHOA DOWN:
A golfer's cry for his or her putt to stop rolling.

WIND DIAL

WHO'S AWAY OR OUT:
This term refers to the player who is farthest from the ball and therefore has the right to hit next. It is most often used on the green to determine the order for putting.

WIFFLE BALLS:
Plastic balls used for practice.

WIND DIAL:
A visual aid to help identify the direction of the wind. Also called **WIND COMPASS**.

WIFFLE BALLS

WINDCHEATER:
A low drive. A shot that is hit solidly and low into the wind. Also called **BLUE DARTER**. Similar to the **PUNCH SHOT**.

WINDMILL HOLE:
A poorly designed hole.

WINDUP:
The rotation of the body during the golf swing. The movement of the body or a body part around a fixed axis. Most commonly used to describe the body turn around the spine in the full backswing. Also referred to as a **PIVOT, SHOULDER TURN** and **COIL**.

WINTER GREEN:
Temporary greens cut out of the fairway to protect the normal greens during the winter months. These temporary greens are not groomed as thoroughly as the normal greens. Winter greens allow many courses that would normally be forced to close during the winter to remain open. This is more commonly called a temporary green.

WINTER RULES:

A set of rules used in the off season. Special local rules that allow a golfer to improve the position of his or her ball on the fairway.

WIRE TO WIRE:

To lead a tournament in scoring from beginning to end.

WOLF:

Golf game that can be played in threesomes and foursomes. One player is selected to be Wolf off the first tee. Then the Wolf changes each hole. Each player is Wolf four times until the 17th and 18th holes. Points are calculated for all players after each hole. if the Wolf and his partner wins low ball they win the point. If the hole is tied, no points are scored.

WOOD:

The club made of wood or metal heads, used to drive and hit off the fairway. They are associated with distance.

WOODIE:

Woodie is an expression used to describe when a golfer hits a tree with the ball and still manages to par the hole. Where on the tree the ball hits (the trunk, branch, leaves, or limb) makes no difference.

WOODPECKER:

A shot hit into the woods that bounces off a few trees.

WORK THE BALL:

To hit the ball in any direction on demand or preference.

WORM BURNER:

A low mis-hit or a low line drive. A shot that is hit solidly and low to the ground or bouncing along the ground. Also called **GROUNDER**.

WRIST COCK:

The hinging of the wrists during the swing.

WRONG BALL:

Any ball that is not the ball in play by the golfer who hits or plans to hit. A wrong ball is any ball other than a player's ball in play or his/her provisional ball.

WRY NECK:

Club with a curved neck.

WRIST COCK

X:
The mark you put on the scorecard when you do not finish the hole.

X OUT BALLS:
Discount balls due to factory overruns or cosmetic blemishes. A good buy.

YANK:
A putt that is pulled to the left.

YARDAGE (DISTANCE) CHART:
A plan of the holes on a course showing the distance from one point to another. It can be printed by the course or prepared by the golfer or his caddie.

YARDAGE MARKER:
This is a marker that indicates the distance to the green for each of the color blocks off the tee.

YARDAGE RATING:
The rate of the difficulty in playing a hole based on yardage alone.

YELLOW STAKES:
Indicates a water hazard. Not the same as a lateral water hazard.

YIP:
When a golfer misses a short putt because of nerves.

YIPS:
Shakiness or nervousness in making a shot.

YIPS PUTT:
A makable putt in a nervous situation.

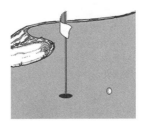

YIPS PUTT

YOU'RE DANCING:
Refers to when a golfer's ball has landed on the green.

ZIP CODE HITTER:

A long ball hitter. A golfer who hits the ball so far it is said to land in the next zip code.

ZIPPER:

A fast swing.

ZONE:

When everything you do is right, and you know it is right. You are at the top of your game.

ZOYSIA:

A warm climate grass with course blades that can handle extreme temperature change.

APPENDIX - GOLFER'S RESOURSES

U.S. SPECIALIZED AND SERVICE GOLF ASSOCIATIONS

U.S MAJOR WORLD ASSOCIATIONS

U.S. NATIONAL GOLF ASSOCIATIONS BY STATE

U.S. MAJOR WOMEN'S GOLF ASSOCIATIONS

U.S. WOMEN'S GOLF ASSOCIATIONS BY STATE

U.S. MAJOR JUNIOR'S GOLF ASSOCIATIONS

U.S. JUNIOR'S GOLF ASSOCIATIONS BY STATE

MAJOR INTERNATIONAL GOLF ASSOCIATIONS

INTERNATIONAL GOLF ASSOCIATIONS BY COUNTRY

U.S. SPECIALIZED AND SERVICE ASSOCIATIONS

PGA World Golf Hall of Fame
P.O. Box 1908
Pinehurst, N.C. 28374
Phone: 919-295-6651

Family Golf Association
2 East Broad St.
Hopewell, NJ 08525
(800) 811-4FGA (4342)
In NJ (609) 466-8348
Executive Director: Larry Sanford
Assistant Director: Whip Burks

United States Blind Golfers Association
c/o Pat W. Browne Jr.
325 Carondelet St.
New Orleans, La. 70130
Phone: 504-522-3203

Minority Golf Association of America,
7705 Georgia Avenue N.W.
Suite 212, Washington, DC 20012
Tel. (202) 829-0596 Or (516) 288-8255

American Singles Golf Association
ASGA National Headquarters
P.O. Box 470493
Charlotte, North Carolina
28247-0493
Telephone: (704) 543-4200
Toll Free: 1-888-GOLFMATE
Fax: (704) 543-7779
TOLL FREE 1-888-465-3628
Toll Free Voice Mail: 1-800-599-2815

National Amputee Golf Association
c/o Bob Wilson
Box 1228
Amherst, N.H. 03031
Phone: 603-673-1135

American Junior Golf Association
2415 Steeplechase Lane
Roswell, Ga. 30076
Phone: 404-998-4653

**American Society of Golf
Course Architects**
221 N. LaSalle St.
Chicago, Ill. 60601
Phone: 312-372-7090

**Golf Course Superintendents
Association of America**
1412 Research Park Dr.
Lawrence, Kan. 66049
Phone: 913-841-2240

National Golf Association
1625 I St. N.W.
Washington, D.C. 20006
Phone: 202-625-2080

**Club Managers
Association of America**
1733 King St.
Alexandria, Va. 22313
Phone: 703-739-9500

National Golf Foundation
1150 South U.S. Hwy. 1
Jupiter, Fla. 33477
Phone: 407-744-6006

Golf Writers Assoc. of America
P.O. Box 328054
Farmington Hills, Mich. 48332
Phone: 313-442-1481

**New Zealand
Under 23 Championship**
Phillip Aickin,
P.O. Box 11-842, Wellington
New Zealand
Ph.: 64 4 472-2967,
Fax: 64 4 499 7330

MAJOR US WORLD GOLF ASSOCIATIONS

U.S.G.A.
World Amateur Golf Council
Golf House
P.O. Box 708
Far Hills, NJ 07931-0708
Tel. 908-234-2300
Fax 908-234-2178

PGA OF AMERICA
Jim Awtrey, , President
Executive Director Tom Addis
P.O. Box 109601
Palm Beach Gardens, FL 33410
or
100 Avenue of the Champions
 Palm Beach Gardens, FL 33418
(407) 624-8400
(800) 4PGA-PRO

PGA Tour
(PGA, Senior PGA, Nike Tours)
112 TPC Blvd., Sawgrass
Ponte Verde Beach Fla. 32082
Phone: 904-285-3700

LPGA TOUR
2570 W. International Speedway B,
Suite B
Daytona Beach, Florida 32111-1118
Tel.: (904) 254-8800
WebSite:
http://www.lpga.com/tour/index.html
E-mail: info@lpga.com

Senior Pga Tour
112 TPC Boulevard
Ponte Vedra Beach, Florida 32082
Tel.: (904) 285-3700
WebSite: http://www.pgatour.com/

Pga Travel
3680 North Peachtree Road
Atlanta, GA 30341
(800) 283-4653 (General Travel)
(800) 868-8337 (Members
Preference)

Executive Women's Golf Assoc.
EWG
P.O. Box 64737-491
Los Angeles, CA 90064
Tel: (310) 335-5446

US NATIONAL GOLF ASSOCIATIONS BY STATE

ALABAMA

Alabama Golf Association
Mr. Buford McCarty
Mailing address:
P.O. Box 660149
Birmingham, AL 35266
Email:bamaga@e-pages.com
webpage: www.e-pages.com/aga
Street address:
1025 Montgomery Highway, Suite 210
Birmingham, AL 35216
205-979-4653
FAX: 205-979-1602

ALASKA

Alaska Golf Association
Mr. Rich Dean
1307 E. 74th Avenue
Anchorage, AK 99518
907-349-4653
FAX: 907-349-6921
or
Mr. Lowell Baumann
Executive Director
Post Office Box 112210
Anchorage AK
 99511-6921
Phone:907-349-6921

ARIZONA

Arizona Golf Association
Mr. Ed Gowan
7226 N. 16th St., Suite 200
Phoenix, AZ 85020
602-944-3035
FAX: 602-944-3228
Email:azgolf@usga.org

ARKANSAS

Arkansas State Golf Association
Mr. Jay Fox
3 Eagle Hill Ct, Ste B
Little Rock, AR 72209
501-455-2742
FAX: 501-455-8111
Email:arkgolf@usga.org
www.argolf.com
or
23111 Biscayne Drive, Suite 206
Little Rock, AR 72207
501-227-8555
FAX: 501-227-8234

CALIFORNIA

Northern California Golf Association
Dennis Davenport
P.O. Box NCGA
3200 Lopez Road)
Pebble Beach, CA 93953
408-625-4653
FAX: 408-625-0150
Email:helen@ncga.org
www.ncga.org

Southern California Golf Association
Mr. Ray Tippet
3740 Cahuenga Blvd., Ste 100
North Hollywood, CA 91604
818-980-3630
FAX: 818-980-5019
or
Mr. Tom Morgan, Exec. Dir.
3740 Cahuenga Boulevard, Suite 100
North Hollywood   CA 91609
Phone:818-980-3630
Fax:818-980-2709
Email:bthomas@scga.org
www.scga.org

US NATIONAL GOLF ASSOCIATIONS BY STATE

CALIFORNIA (cont.)

**Southern California Public Links
Golf Association**
Mr. James Dout
7035 Orangethorpe Ave., Suite E
Buenna Park, CA 90621
714-994-4747
FAX: 714-994-5407

Western American Golf Association
Linda Garrison, President
1181 N. Diamond Bar Boulevard
Diamond Bar, CA 91765
E-Mail: westernga@usga.org
805-482-3994
or
Handicap Chairman:
Clarice Olive
1181 Pebble Beach
Upland, CA 91784
909-946-9693
or
Handicap Chairman:
Dorsey Gale
2429 Alcott Court
San Diego, CA 92106
619-221-0848

Cal Poly Golf Association
1 Polytechnic Way
San Luis Obispo, CA 93410
805-756-4418

Western States Golf Association
Mr. William Clark
2815 Somerset Drive
Los Angeles, CA 90016
213-737-0249

COLORADO

Colorado Golf Association
Col. Warren Simmons
5655 S. Yosemite Street, Suite 101
Englewood, CO 80111
303-779-4653
Fax: 303-228-4675
E-mail: cologolf@usga.org

CONNECTICUT

Connecticut State Golf Assoction
Delmore Kinney, Jr.
35 Cold Spring Road, Ste. 212
Rocky Hill, CT 06067
860-257-4171
Fax: 860-257-8355
Email:ctstate@usga.org
www.ctgolfer.com/csga
or
Mr. James E. Sweeney
35 Cold Spring Road
Rocky Hill, CT 06067
806-257-4171
Fax: 806-257-8355

DELAWARE

Delaware State Golf Association
Mr. J. Curtis Riley
7234 Lancaster Pike, Suite 302B
Hockessin, DE 19707
302-234-3365
Fax: 302-234-3359
Email:dsga@usga.org
www.golfnet.com/dsga/dsga.htp

US NATIONAL GOLF ASSOCIATIONS BY STATE

DISTRICT OF COLUMBIA

**Washington Metropolitan
Golf Association**
Mr. Robert Riley III
5904 Mt. Eagle Dr. Unit 310
Alexandria, VA 22303
703-329-3989
FAX 703-329-1013
or
8012 Colorado Springs Drive
Springfield, VA 22153
703-569-6311
or
Course Rating:
Mr. Ed Dosek
1566 Farlow Avenue
Crofton, MD 21114
410-721-2565

FLORIDA

PGA OF AMERICA
Jim Awtrey, , President
Executive Director Tom Addis
P.O. Box 109601
 Palm Beach Gardens, FL 33410
or
100 Avenue of the Champions
 Palm Beach Gardens, FL 33418
(407) 624-8400
(800) 4PGA-PRO

PGA Tour
(PGA, Senior PGA, Nike Tours)
112 TPC Blvd., Sawgrass
Ponte Verde Beach Fla. 32082
Phone: 904-285-3700

Senior Pga Tour
112 TPC Boulevard
Ponte Vedra Beach, Florida 32082
Tel.: (904) 285-3700
WebSite: http://www.pgatour.com/

FLORIDA (cont.)

Golf Association of Florida
Charlie Stein
P.O. Box 838
Lake Hamilton, FL 33851
941-439-3111
FAX: 941-439-4286

Florida State Golf Association
Mr. Jim Demick
5714 Draw Lane
Sarasota, FL 34238
941-921-5695
Fax: 941-923-1254
Email:fsga@usga.org
www.fsga.org
or
Mr. Cal Korf
Mailing address:
P.O. Box 21177
Sarasota, FL 34276
Street address:
5710 Draw Lane
Sarasota, FL 34238
813-921-5695
Fax: 813-923-1254

GEORGIA

Pga Travel
3680 North Peachtree Road
Atlanta, GA 30341
(800) 283-4653 (General Travel)
(800) 868-8337 (Members Preference)

Georgia State Golf Association
Mr. Mike Waldron
121 Village Parkway, Bldg. 3
Marietta, GA 30067
770-955-4272
Fax: 770-955-1156
Email:gsga@usga.org
www.gsga.org

US NATIONAL GOLF ASSOCIATIONS BY STATE

HAWAII

Hawaii State Golf Association
Mr. Paul Wamaschige Exec. Dir.
Paul Tamashige
3599 Waialae Avenue, PH
Honolulu, HI 96816-2759
TEL: 808-732-9785
Fax: 808-735-8097
or
Mr. Jim Hammons
3599 Waialae Avenue, PH
Honolulu, HI 96816-2759
808-732-9785
Fax: 808-735-8097
or
Mrs. Bev Kim
Exec. Dir.
350-D Kaelepulu Drive
Kailua, HI   96734
Tel: 808-262-2428

IDAHO

Idaho Golf Association
Vicky Davis
Mailing address:
P.O. Box 3025
Boise, ID 83703
208-342-4442
FAX: 208-345-5959
or
Mr. V. Lyman Gallup
P.O. Box 3025
Boise, ID 83703
Street address:
4048 Chinden Blvd., Suite 203
Boise, ID 83714
208-342-4442
Email:idahoga@usga.org

ILLINOIS

Chicago District Golf Association
Mr. Robert Markionni
Executive Director
619 Enterprize Drive, Suite 204
Oak Brook, IL 60521
630-954-2180
Fax: 630-954-3650
Email:cdga1@starnetinc.com
www.cdga.org

Southern Illinois Golf Association
Don E. Johnson, Executive Dir.
1 North Main Street
Pinckneyville, IL 62274
618-357-2178
FAX: 618-357-3314
or
Mr. Bob Kearney
1917 Lake Street
Mt. Vernon, IL 62864
618-244-3826

Western Golf Association
Donald Johnson, Executive Director
1 Briar Road
Golf, IL 60029
708-724-4600
Fax: 708-724-7133

Illinois Section Pga Of America
Mike Miller, Executive Director
2100 Clearwater Drive, Suite 206
Oak Brook, IL 60521
Tel: (708) 990-7799
Fax: (708) 990-7864

US NATIONAL GOLF ASSOCIATIONS BY STATE

INDIANA

Indiana Golf Association
Mr. Matt Brookshire, Exec. Dir.
P. O. Box 516
Franklin, IN 46131
317-738-9696
Fax: 317-738-9436
Email:indianagolfa@usga.org

IOWA

Iowa Golf Association
Mr. Kirk Stanzel
1930 St. Andrews, N.E.
Cedar Rapids, IA 52402
319-378-9142
FAX: 319-378-9203

KANSAS

Kansas Golf Association
Mr. Kim Richey
3301 Clinton Parkway Court, Suite 4
Lawrence, KS 66047
913-842-4833
Fax: 913-842-3831

Kansas City District Golf Association
Mr. Robert Reid
3756 W. 95th St.
Leawood, KS 66206
913-649-5242
FAX: 913-649-4190
or
9331 Ensley Lane
Leawood, KS 66206
913-649-8872
Fax: 913-649-5242

KENTUCKY

Kentucky Golf Association
Mr. Bill Coomer
Tournament Director
P.O. Box 18396
Louisville, KY 40261
Phone:502-499-7255
Fax:502-499-7422
or
Mr. Mike Donahoe
4109 Bardstown Road, Suite 5A
Louisville, KY 40218
502-499-7255
Fax: 502-499-7422

LOUISIANA

Louisiana State Golf Association
Mr. Carr McCalla
Executive Director
1003 Hugh Wallis Road, Suite I
Lafayette, LA 70508
318-265-3938
Fax: 318-234-2197
Email:louisga@usga.org

New Orleans Golf Association
Mr. Owen LeBlanc, President
6480 Airgonne Blvd.
New Orleans, LA 70124
504-488-5106

US NATIONAL GOLF ASSOCIATIONS BY STATE

MAINE

Maine State Golf Association
Nancy S. DeFrancesco, Executive Dir.
Romeo Laberge, Tournament Director
Jane Gildart, Administrative Assistant
374 U.S. Route One
Yarmouth, Maine 04096
207-846-3800
FAX: (207) 846-4055
email: mainegolf@usga.org
or
Mr. Ralph Noel
Mailing address:
P.O. Box 419
Auburn, ME 04212
Street address:
272 Court Street
Auburn, ME 04210
207-795-6742

MARYLAND

Maryland State Golf Association
Mr. John A. Emich
P.O. Box 16289
Baltimore, MD 21210
410-467-8899 (Office)
FAX: 410-467-5729

MASSACHUSETTS

New England Golf Association
Mr. Harry McCracken
175 Highland Ave.
Needham, MA 02192
781-449-3000

MASSACHUSETTS (cont.)

Massachusetts Golf Association
Tom Landry - Executive Director
175 Highland Avenue
Needham, MA 02192
781-449-3000
FAX: 781-449-4020
or
Mr. Richard Haskell
Mailing address:
P.O. Box 55
Newton Lower Falls, MA 02162
Email:kevindp@msn.com
www.massgolf.org
or
Street address:
175 Highland Avenue
Needham, MA 02192
617-449-3000
FAX: 617-449-4020

MICHIGAN

Golf Association of Michigan
Mr. Brett Marshall
37935 Twelve Mile Road, Suite 200A
Farmington Hills, MI 48331
248-553-4200
FAX: 248-553-4438
Email:bmarshal@gam.org
www.gam.org

US NATIONAL GOLF ASSOCIATIONS BY STATE

MINNESOTA

Minnesota Golf Association
Mr. Ross Galarneault
6550 York Avenue, South
Suite 211
Edina, MN 55435
612-927-4643
FAX: 612-927-9642
Email:info.@mngolf.org
www.mngolf.org
or
Course Rating:
Dick Bennett
945 Brisbin St.
Anoka, MN 55303
612-427-1142

MISSISSIPPI

Mississippi Golf Association
Jeff Morton
P.O. Box 2467
Madison, MS 39130-2467
601-853-4160
FAX: 601-856-5580
Email:missga@usga.org
www.msmall.com/missgolf
or
Mr. Bill Cass
Mailing address:
P.O. Box 684
Laurel, MS 39441
or
Street address:
1019 North 12th Avenue, #A3
Laurel, MS 39440
601-649-0570
FAX: 601-649-0570

MISSOURI

St. Louis District Golf Assoc.
Mr. Larry Etzkorn
823 Cleveland
St. Louis, MO 63122
314-821-1511
or
823 Cleveland
Kirkwood, MO 63122
(314) 821-1511

St. Louis Seniors' Golf Association
207 Parchurst Terrace
St. Louis, MO 63119
(314) 962-6417

Missouri Golf Association
Mr. William D. Wells
Mailing address:
P.O. Box 104164
Jefferson City, MO 65110
Email:mogolf@usga.org
or
1808B Southwest Blvd.
Jefferson City, MO 65109
573-636-8994
FAX: 573-636-4225

Metropolitan Amateur Golf Assoc.
Mr. Tom O'Toole, Jr.
2900 S. Brentwood Blvd.
St. Louis, MO 63144
314-961-3300
FAX: 314-961-4425

US NATIONAL GOLF ASSOCIATIONS BY STATE

NEW HAMPSHIRE

New Hampshire Golf Association
Gary Philippy
1650 Elm St. Suite 201
Manchester, NH 03104
603-623-0396
or
Dr. Robert Elliott, Exec. Dir.
45 Kearney Street
Manchester NH 03104
Phone:603-623-0396
or
Mr. John Jelley, Exec. Dir.
Post Office Box 778
Concord NH 03302
Phone:603-228-3089
Fax:603-749-3761
Email:jjelly@ultranet.com
or
Course Rating:
Mr. Nip Lewis
5B Pine Isle Drive
Derry, NH 03038
603-434-4839

NEW JERSEY

New Jersey State Golf Association
Mr. Steve Foehl
1000 Broad Street
Bloomfiefld, NJ 07003
201-338-8334
FAX: 201-338-5525
Email:njsga@usga.org

Metropolitan Golf Association
Mr. Jay Mottola
49 Knollwood Road
Elmsford, NY 10523
914-347-4653
Fax: 914-347-3437

NEW JERSEY (cont.)

South Jersey Golf Association
Arlene Cherwien
336 Highland Ave.
Vineland, NJ 08360
609-691-3737
Fax:609-507-1414
Email:sjga@usga.org
or
Nancy E. Lauber
144 Valley Forge Drive
Tuckerton, NJ 08087
609-296-5048

NEW MEXICO

**Sun Country Amateur
Golf Assoc.**
Mr. J. P. Messick
10035 Country Club Lane NW,
Suite 5
Albuquerque, NM 87114
505-897-0864
FAX: 505-897-3494

US NATIONAL GOLF ASSOCIATIONS BY STATE

NEW YORK

Metropolitan Golf Association
Mr. Jay Mottola
49 Knollwood Road
Elmsford, NY 10523
914-347-4653
Fax: 914-347-3437

Buffalo District Golf Association
Mr. Whitey Nichols
Box 19
Cheektowaga, NY 14225
716-632-1936

Metropolitan Golf Association
Mr. Jay Mottola
49 Knollwood Road
Elmsford, NY 10523
914-347-4653
Fax: 914-347-3437
Email:mgagolf@aol.com

New York State Golf Association
J. Patrick Keenan
P.O. Box 333
Syracuse, NY 13215-0333
315-471-6979
FAX: 315-471-1372
Email:nysga@usga.org
www.nysga.org
or
Mr. Thomas Riedy
P.O. Box 3459
Elmira, NY 14905-0459
607-733-0007 (B)
607-732-6446 (H)

Finger Lakes Golf Association
Mr. Robert Griswold
2380 Fort Hill Road
Phelps, NY 14532

NEW YORK (cont.)

Eastern New York Golf Assoc.
Mr. Earl Feiden, Jr.
29 Spring Street
Loudonville, NY 12211

Syracuse District Golf Association
Mr. John P. Chiasson
129 Shady Lane
Fayetteville, NY 13066
315-637-8200

Rochester District Golf Assoc.
Harold R. Bolles
2060 Brighton-Henrietta Townline Rd.
Rochester, NY 14623
716-292-5950
FAX: 716-292-1259
or
Mr. Richard Van Hook
333 Metro Park, Suite M-110
Rochester, NY 14623
716-292-5950
FAX: 716-292-1259

NORTH CAROLINA

Carolinas Golf Association
Mr. Jack Nance
P.O. Box 319
West End, NC 27376
Street address:
135-B North Trade St.
Seven Lake Village
West End, NC 27376
910-673-1000
Fax: 910-673-1001
Email:cga@thecga.org
www.golfnet.com/cga

US NATIONAL GOLF ASSOCIATIONS BY STATE

NORTH DAKOTA

North Dakota Golf Association
Mr. Steve R. Bain
P.O. Box 452
Bismarck, ND 58502
701-223-2233
FAX: 701-223-0284
Email:sr.bainprodigy.net

OHIO

Ohio Golf Association/Columbus District Golf Association
James M. Popa, Executive Director
4701 Olentangy River Rd. #200A
Columbus, OH 43214
614-457-8169
FAX: 614-457-8211

Greater Cincinnati Golf Assoc.
Mr. Tay Baker
Mailing address:
P.O. Box 317825
Street address:
1043 Eastgate Drive
Cincinnati, OH 45231
513-521-4242
Fax:same # press *
Email:www.cincyga@usga.org
www.cincygolf.com

Northern Ohio Golf Association
Mr. Robert A. Wharton
10210 Brecksville Road
Brecksville, OH 44141
216-838-8733
FAX: 216-838-8739
Email:noga@usga.org

OHIO (cont.)

Columbus District Golf Association
Mr. James Popa
5300 McKitrick Blvd.
Columbus, OH 43235
614-457-8169
FAX: 614-457-8211
or
Course Rating:
Mr. Duane Guerin
1840 Ardleigh Rd.
Columbus, OH 43221
614-457-0512
or
Dr. Fred Balthaser
437 Pamlico
Columbus, OH 43228

Miami Valley Golf Association
Steve Jurick, Executive Director
c/o Dayton Country Club
555 Kramer Road
Dayton, OH 45419
937-294-6842
FAX: 937-294-7003

Toledo District Golf Association
Mrs. Marianne Reece
5533 Southwyck Blvd., Suite 204
Toledo, OH 43614
419-866-4771
FAX: 419-866-0388
Email:tdga@usga.org
or
Mrs. Pam Brazeau
2313 Rockspring Court
Toledo, OH 43614
419-866-8795

Akron District Golf Association
Larry Horner
P.O. Box 14
Cuyahoga Falls, OH 44221

US NATIONAL GOLF ASSOCIATIONS BY STATE

OKLAHOMA

Oklahoma State Golf Association
Mr. Rick Coe
Mailing address:
P.O. Box 13590
Oklahoma City, OK 73113
Street address:
6217 N. Classen Blvd.
Oklahoma City, OK 73118
405-848-0042
FAX: 405-840-9435

OREGON

Oregon Golf Association
Mr. James Gibbons
8364 S.W. Nimbus Avenue, Ste A1
Beaverton, OR 97008
503-643-2610
FAX: 503-641-6795
Email:gibbons@orgolf.org
www.orgolf.org

PENNSYLVANIA

Anthracite Golf Association
Mr. Dennis Corvo
617 Keystone Avenue
Peckville, PA 18452
717-489-4711

Erie District Golf Association
Dr. Richard M. Marasco
3319 Liberty St.
Erie, PA 16508
814 866-2195
FAX: 814 474-1703
or
Mr. David O. Hewett
1223 Jonathan Drive
Erie, PA 16510
814-825-9051

PENNSYLVANIA (cont.)

York County Amateur Golf Assoc.
Mr. Gary Sutton
Mailing address:
P.O. Box 193
Street address:
2940 Honey Valley Road
Dallastown, PA 17313
717-741-2432
FAX: 717-741-2432

Golf Association of Philadelphia
Mr. James D. Sykes
Mailing address:
Drawer 808
Southeastern, PA 19399-0808
Street address:
700 Croton Road
Wayne, PA 19087
610-687-2340
FAX: 610-687-2082

Western Pennsylvania Golf Assoc.
Mr. Jeff Rivard
324 4th Street
Pittsburgh, PA 15238
412-826-2180
FAX: 412-826-2183
Email:westpennga@usga.org

North Central Pennsylvania Golf Association
Jeff Ranck
425 S. 21st St.
Lewisburg, PA 17837
717-523-3552
FAX: 717-522-0408
or
Mr. Dennis Clark
RD #3, Box 48
Mifflintown, PA 17059
717-463-2111
FAX: 717-522-0408

US NATIONAL GOLF ASSOCIATIONS BY STATE

PENNSYLVANIA (cont.)

Keystone Public Golf Association
Ms. Lois Sparrow
Mailing address:
P.O. Box 399
Export, PA 15632
Street address:
2186 Locust Street
Export, PA 15632
412-468-8850
FAX: 412-468-8897

PUERTO RICO

Puerto Rico Golf Association
Mr. James Teale, Exec. Dir.
GPO Box 363862
SanJuan PR   936
Phone:787-781-2070
Fax:787-781-2210

RHODE ISLAND

Rhode Island Golf Association
Mr. Joseph Sprague
10 Orms Street, Suite 326
Providence, RI 02904
401-272-1350
FAX: 401-331-3627

SOUTH CAROLINA

South Carolina Golf Association
Mr. Happ Lathrop
Mailing address:
P.O. Box 286
Street address:
7451 Irmo Drive
Irmo, SC 29063
803-732-9311
FAX: 803-732-7406
Email:scarolinagolf@usga.org
www.golfnet.com/scga

SOUTH DAKOTA

South Dakota Golf Association
Mr. Tom Egan
Executive Director
P.O. Box 88414
Sioux Falls   SD 57105
Phone:605-338-7499
Fax:605-338-2865
Email:sdga@usga.org
or
Jay Huizenga
P.O. Box 88414
Sioux Falls, SD 57109
605-338-7499
FAX: 605-338-2865

TENNESSEE

Tennessee Golf Association
Mr. Dick Horton
400 Franklin Rd.
Franklin, TN 37069
615-790-7600
FAX: 615-790-8600
Email:tennga@usga.org

US NATIONAL GOLF ASSOCIATIONS BY STATE

TEXAS

Houston Golf Association
Mr. Patrick Fitzpatrick, President
1830 South Millbend Drive
The Woodlands TX 77380
Phone:713-367-7999
Fax:281-363-9888
Email:office@hga.org
www.shellhoustonpen.com

Dallas District Golf Association
Mr. Chuck Ashmore
381 Casa Linda Plaza #375
Dallas, TX 75218
214-823-6004

San Antonio Golf Association
Tony Piazzi
P.O. Box 791604
San Antonio, TX 78279
2929 Mossrock Suite 117
San Antonio, TX 78230

Southern Texas Golf Association
Patrick Fitspatrick
1830 S. Millbend Drive
The Woodlands, TX 77380
281-367-7999
FAX: 281-363-9888
or
Mr. Eric Fredrickson
1830 S. Millbend Drive
The Woodlands, TX 77380
713-367-7999

Texas Golf Association
Mr. William A. Penn
1000 Westbank Drive
Austin, TX 78746
512-328-4653
FAX: 512-328-4653

TEXAS (cont.)

Northern Texas Golf Association
Mr. Donald R. Brown
6426 Covecreek Place
Dallas, TX 75240-5452
972-386-6842
Fax: 972-386-6843
E-mail: ntga@ntga.org
Email:donbrown@ntga.org

UTAH

Utah Golf Association
Mr. Joe Watts
1110 E. Eaglewood Drive
North Salt Lake City, UT 84054
801-299-8421
Fax: 801-299-9409
Email:uga@usga.com
www.uga.org

VERMONT

Vermont Golf Association
Mr. Jim Bassett
Mailing address:
P.O. Box 1612, Station A
Rutland, VT 05701
Street address:
c/o Rutland Country Club
North Grove Street
Rutland, VT 05701
802-773-7180
FAX: 802-773-7182

US NATIONAL GOLF ASSOCIATIONS BY STATE

VIRGINIA

Virginia State Golf Association
Mr. David A. Norman
830 South Lake Blvd. Ste A
Richmond, VA 23236
804-378-2300
FAX: 804-378-2369
E-mail danorman@msn.com
Email:info@vsga.org
www.vsga.org
or
Course Rating:
Mr. Wallace McDowell
P.O. Box 5527
Charlottesville, VA 22901

Washington Metro Golf Association
Mr. Robert Riley III, Exec. Dir.
5904 Mount Eagle Drive #310
Alexandria VA 22303
Phone:703-329-3989

**Tournament Golf
Association of Virginia**
7892 Virginia Oaks Drive
Gainseville, VA 20155-2835
800-929-7449
FAX: 703-754-8285
info@virginiatga.com

WASHINGTON

**Washington State Golf Association
(Pacific Northwest Golf Association)**
Mr. John Bodenhamer
Northgate Executive Center I
155 N.E. 100th Street, Suite 302
Seattle, WA 98125
206-526-1238
FAX: 206-522-0281
Email:washga@usga.org

WEST VIRGINIA

West Virginia Golf Association
Danny Fisher
P. O. Box 850
Hurricane, WV 25526-0850
304-757-3444
FAX: 304-757-3479
Email:wvga@usga.org
or
Mr. William Dickens
3744 Teays Valley Road, Suite 208
Hurricane, WV 25526-0870
304-757-3444
FAX: 304-757-3479

WISCONSIN

Wisconsin State Golf Association
Mr. Eugene R. Haas
Mailing address:
P.O. Box 35
Elm Grove, WI 53122
414-786-4301
FAX: 414-786-4202

WYOMING

Wyoming State Golf Association
Mr. Jim Core, Executive Director
500 8th Avenue North
Greybull, WY 82426
307-568-3304 or 307-765-2345

Wyoming State Golf Association
Ms. Diana Johnson, Executive Sec.
1808 Kit Carson
Casper, WY 82604
307-265-8445
Fax: 307-265-0668

MAJOR US WOMAN'S NATIONAL ASSOCIATIONS

Executive Women's Golf Association
EWG
P.O. Box 64737-491
Los Angeles, CA 90064
Tel: (310) 335-5446

Pacific Women's Golf Association
2542 S. Bascom Ave.
Suite 117, Campbell, CA 95008
Office Manager : Caroline O'Brien
408 377-2430 or (800) 995-7942
FAX: (408) 377-0735
EMAIL: pacwomensga@usga.org

Western American Golf Association
WAGA
929 E. Foothill Blvd., #150
Upland, CA 91786
Phone: (909) 920-0056
Fax: (909) 931-3988
E-mail: westernga@usga.org

South American Wpga
WPGA
Box 52631
Saxonwold, 2132,
South Africa
Office phone - 027 11 646 5702
FAX number - 027 11 646 5715
Email : lesley@pinksoft.co.za

Women's Southern California
Golf Associations
WSCGA
402 W. Arrow Hwy, Suite 10
San Dimas, CA 91773
Phone : 909-592-1281
FAX : 909-592-7542
E-mail : wscga@womensgolf.org

Ladies Professional Golf Assoc.
LPGA.
All content.
100 International Golf Dr.
Daytona Beach, FL 32124-1092
Phone: (904) 274-6200
Fax: (904) 274-1099

Women's Nine Hole Golf Assoc.
WNHGA
Contact: President:
Donna Okamoto: (408) 253-4440
Secretary:
Anne Hoak: (209) 533-0326

Women's Golf Association
Of Northern California
WGANC
Mary Mahaney, Executive Dir.
5776 Stoneridge Mall Rd, #160
Pleasanton, California 94588
Telephone: (925) 737-0963
FAX: (925) 737-0964
E-mail: wganc@usga.org

US WOMENS GOLF ASSOCIATIONS BY STATE

ALABAMA

Women's Alabama Golf Association
Mrs. Janie Soloman
Executive Director
403 North Cherokee
Dothan, AL 36303
334-794-6491
FAX: 334-794-6491
or
Mrs. Mary Dean Gray, President
2700 Arlington Crest, #10
Birmingham, AL 35205
205-933-8836

ALASKA - No listing

ARIZONA

Arizona Women's Golf Association
Mr. Jamie D. Wagner
141 East Palm Lane #210
Phoenix, AZ 85004
602-253-5655
FAX: 602-253-6210
or
Ms. Janice F. Era
7226 N. 16th St., Suite 200
Phoenix, AZ 85020
602-944-9114
FAX: 602-943-8414

ARKANSAS

Arkansas Women's Golf Association
Mrs Pennie Barlow, President
39 Kensington Drive
Conway, AR 72032
501-329-7338
or
P.O. Box 562
Monticello, AR 71657
870-538-3771

CALIFORNIA

**Women's Golf Association
of Northern California**
Mrs. Kaytee Lively
1768 Coniferious, P.O. Box 2024
Arnold, CA 95223
209-795-0220
or
Mrs. June Larrick
44 W. Douglas Avenue
Visalia, CA 23291
209-635-8477

Pacific Women's Golf Association
Caroline O'Brien, Office Manager
2542 South Bason Ave., Suite 117
Campbell, CA 95008
408-377-2430
Email: pacswomensga@usga.org
or
Ms. Micki Willey, Office Manager
1471 Industrial Avenue
San Jose, CA 95112
408-995-0340
FAX: 408-294-6960

**Women's Southern California
Golf Association**
Ms. Pat Blalock, Executive Director
402 W. Arrow Highway, Suite 10
San Dimas, CA 91773
909-592-1281
FAX: 909-592-7542
Email:wscga@womensgolf.org
www.womensgolf.org
Course Rating: Judy Borden

**Women's Golf Association
of Northern California**
Mrs. June Larrick, President
44 W. Douglas Avenue
Visalia, CA 23291
209-635-8477

US WOMENS GOLF ASSOCIATIONS BY STATE

CALIFORNIA (cont.)

Women's Public Links Golf Association of Southern California
437 Eucalyptus Drive
Redlands, CA 92373
909-793-0402
or
Diana Quint, President
3647 Poe Street
San Diego, CA 92106
619-222-9166

San Diego Women's Golf Association
9933 Meadow Glen Way East
Escondido, CA 92026
760-749-1190
or
Rosemarie Kohler, President
2316 Azure Lane
Vista, CA 92083
619-598-9211
or
Handicap Chairman:
Dorsey Gale
2429 Alcott Court
San Diego, CA 92106
619-221-0848

Women's Nine Hole Golf Association
Ms. Ruth Benzing, President
20297 Ljepava
Saratoga, CA 95070
408-867-0462

COLORADO

Colorado Women's Golf Association
Mrs. Robin Elbardawil, Executive Dir.
Kathy Roady, President
5655 S. Yosemite Street, Suite 101
Englewood, CO 80111
303-220-5456
Fax: 303-290-0593
E-mail: cowga@usga.org

CONNECTICUT

Connecticut Women's Golf Assoc.
Ginger Broadbent
2195 Shepard Avenue
Mt. Carmel, CT 06518
203-281-3913
or
Course Rating:
Jane B. Witherwax
120 Hurds Hill Road
Woodbury, CT 06798

Connecticut Women's Golf Assoc.
Mrs. Linda Kaye
27 Hunter Road
Avon,CT 06001
203-678-0380
Course Rating:
Jane B. Witherwax
120 Hurds Hill Road
Woodbury, CT 06798

Southern New England Women's Golf Association
Jenny Burrill
8 Farmington Chase
Farmington, CT 86032
860-547-3205
or
Mrs. Miki Marks,
5 Ranch Drive
Trumbull, CT 06611
203-268-2519
or
Mrs. Betty Holden, President
7 Crane Place
Simsbury, CT 06070
860-658-6330

US WOMENS GOLF ASSOCIATIONS BY STATE

DELAWARE

Delaware Women's Golf Assoc.
Ms. Debbie Ryan, Operations Man.
P.O. Box 15107
Newark, DE 19711
302-995-6765
or
Mrs. Kay Henry, President
542 Cabot Drive
Hockessin, DE 19707
302-239-4753

DISTRICT OF COLUMBIA

**Women's District of Columbia
Golf Association**
Rose Marie Vargo
6424 Wiscasset Road
Bethesda, MD 20816
301-229-7056
FAX: 301-229-7043
or
Ms. Nancy Graves
2328 S. Nash Street
Arlington, VA 22202
703-979-3766

FLORIDA

LPGA TOUR
2570 W. International Speedway B,
Suite B
Daytona Beach, Florida 32111-1118
Tel.: (904) 254-8800
WebSite:
http://www.lpga.com/tour/index.html
E-mail: info@lpga.com

FLORIDA (cont.)

Florida Women's State Golf Assoc.
Judy Comella, Executive Director
10000 N U.S. Highway 98 #107
Lakeland, FL 33809
1-888-GOLF997
Email:fwsga@usga.org
or
Mrs. Betty Scott Forbes, President
1311 S.W. Briarwood Drive
Port St. Lucie, FL 34986
407-879-9642

Florida Women's Golf Association
Mrs. Florence Godino
Past President
3304 Pebble Beach Drive
Lake Worth FL 33467
Phone:561-964-2629
Email:FGODINO@aol.com

GEORGIA

Pga Travel
3680 North Peachtree Road
Atlanta, GA 30341
(800) 283-4653 (General Travel)
(800) 868-8337 (Members Preference)

Georgia Women's Golf Association
Mrs. Janie Holt
Executive Director
426 Flat Creek Trail
Fayetteville
GA
Zip:30214
Phone:770-487-2628

US WOMENS GOLF ASSOCIATIONS BY STATE

HAWAII

Hawaii State Women's Golf Assoc.
Ms. Kathy Ordway
350-D Kaelepulu Drive
Kailua, HI 96734
808-262-2428
or
Mrs. Sally Harper
1025 Wilder Ave, Apt. 8B
Honolulu, HI 96822
808-536-0157
or
Course Rating:
Joie Gopez
125 E. Maunalua St.
Honolulu, HI 96821
808-395-5933

IDAHO

Idaho Golf Association
Vicky Davis
Mailing address:
P.O. Box 3025
Boise, ID 83703
208-342-4442
FAX: 208-345-5959

ILLINOIS

Illinois Section Pga Of America
Mike Miller, Executive Director
2100 Clearwater Drive, Suite 206
Oak Brook, IL 60521
Tel: (708) 990-7799
Fax: (708) 990-7864

ILLINOIS (cont.)

**Chicago Women's District
Golf Association**
Mrs. Dorothy Banas
430 Chapel Hill Lane
Northfield, IL 60093
847-446-7622
or
Mrs. Lorraine Scodro
7447 Menitoba Avenue
Champaign, IL 61821
708-448-5224

Illinois Women's Golf Association
Mrs. Judy Mott , Exec. Dir.
1731 National Avenue
Rockford IL   61103

**Southern Illinois Ladies
Golf Association**
Mrs. Leeann Grief
3840 State Highway 14
Mulkeytown, IL 62865
618-724-2471

INDIANA

Indiana Women's Golf Association
Mrs. Jan Woschitz
72 Beauvoir Circle
Anderson, IN 46011
or
Mrs. Cinda Brown
930 North Morgan Street
Rushville, IN 47421
317-938-5273
or
Mrs. Julie Carmichael , Exec. Dir.
1 American Square , Suite 2245
Indianapolis , IN 46282
Fax:317-692-5233

US WOMENS GOLF ASSOCIATIONS BY STATE

IOWA

Iowa Women's Golf Association
Trudie Higgs
2605 Linda Drive
Des Moines, IA 50322-5209
515-276-3622
or
Ms. Corrine Nydle, President
2107 Birchwood Drive, N.E.
Cedar Rapids, IA 52402
319-393-9370
or
Course Rating:
Diane Kasdorf
2205 Crown Flalr Dr.
Des Moines, IA 50265

KANSAS

Kansas Women's Golf Association
Natasha Fife
5701 E. 19th Street N.
Wichita, KS 67208
Email:nfife@prodigy.net
or
Ms. Rosemary Ralston
1213 Neosho
Emporia, KS 66801
316-342-8582
Fax: 316-263-5301

KENTUCKY - No listing

LOUISIANA

**New Orleans Women's
Golf Association**
Mrs. Patricia Ingels
3624 Audubon Trace
Jefferson, LA 70121
Phone:504-833-7046

LOUISIANA (cont.)

**New Orleans Women's
Golf Association**
Mrs. Brenda Kahan
3517 Lake Kristin Drive
Gretna, LA 70056
504-394-6310

**Louisiana Women's State
Golf Association**
Mitzy Morgan
3257 Debra Dr.
Monroe, LA 71201
318-325-6828
or
Mrs. Judy Roberts
9948 Beaver Creek Drive
Shreveport, LA 71106
318-797-6476
or
Course Rating:
Juanita Dryant
P.O. Box 55
Porte Barre LA 70577
318-585-6479

MAINE

Women's Maine State Golf Assoc.
Mrs. Diane Johnson
323 West Road
West Gardner, ME 04345
or
Ms. Debbie Cianchette
33 Scrimshaw Lane
Saco, ME 04072
207-282-1467

**Southern Maine Women's
Golf Association**
Ms. Lyn Mann, Executive Director
128 Warren Avenue
Portland, ME 04103

US WOMENS GOLF ASSOCIATIONS BY STATE

MAINE (cont.)

Southern Maine Women's Golf Association

Mrs. Shirley Davenport, President
P. O. Box 15
York, ME 03909
207-363-2252
or
Course Rating:
Pauline G. Raymond
15 Delcliff Lane
Lewiston, ME 04240

MARYLAND

Maryland State Golf Assoc. Women's Division
Pat Kaufman, President
1205 Swan Harbour Circle
Fort Washington, MD 20744
301-292-2345

Women's Golf Association of Baltimore
Glena Wirtanen
3810 Bleheim Rd.
Phoenix, MD 21131
or
Ms. Lucy Preston
2 Nearfield Road
Lutherville, MD 21093
410-296-3316

MASSACHUSETTS

Massachusetts Women's Golf Association
Ms. Sally Fish, President
175 Highland Avenue
Needham   MA   02192
Phone:617-891-4200

MASSACHUSETTS (cont.)

New England Women's Golf Assoc.
Mrs. Sidney Arnold, Exec. Sec.
P.O. Box 1377
Duxbury, MA 02331
617-934-2425

Women's Golf Association of Massachusetts
Ms. Janice Vance, Executive Director
6 Kings Road
Lynnfield, MA 01940
781-453-0555
FAX: 781-453-0827
or
Ms. Ann Marie Tobin, President
36 Locksley Road
Lynnfield, MA 01940
617-334-6047
Course Rating: Suzanne Nelson

**SAWGA
Stow Acres Women's Golf Assoc.**
Ms. Renee M. Fraser, President
127 Rand Terrace
Newton, MA 02466
617-969-5685

**SWING
Sporting Women's Invitational Golf**
Mary E. Porter, President
P.O. Box 225
Whitman, MA 02382
781-447-2299

US WOMENS GOLF ASSOCIATIONS BY STATE

MICHIGAN

**Women's District Golf
Association of Detroit**
Linda Lester
1353 Blairmoor CT.
Grosse Pointe Woods, MI 48236
or
Ms. Trish Young
2760 MacIntosh Lane
Bloomfield Hills, MI 48302
810-828-4623

MINNESOTA

Minnesota Women's Golf Assoc.
Ms. Nancy Messerli
4795 Bayswater Road
Shorewood, MN 55331
612-474-6162
or
Mrs. Ede Rice
4801 Hilltop Lane
Edina, MN 55424
612-927-8372

MISSISSIPPI

Mississippi Women's Golf Assoc.
Mrs. Jerrie White
434 Forest Lake Place
Madison, MS 39110
or
Mrs. Lisa Parris
809 Oak Trail
Canton, MS 39046
601-856-1627
or
Course Rating:
Lou Garick
2811 Pecan Ridge Rd.
Laurel, MS 39440

MISSOURI

**St. Louis Women's District
Golf Association**
Sharon Dillaha, President
1008 Picardy Lane
St. Charles, MO 63301
314-947-7291
or
Mrs. JoEllen Montgomery
61 Muirfield
St. Louis, MO 63141
(314) 434-2762
or
Ms. Lucinn Sams
2359 Baxton Way
Chesterfield, MO 63017
314-394-5641
or
Course Rating:
Jayne Watson
13 Brook Mill Lane
Chesterfield, MO 63017
314-434-2074

Missouri Women's Golf Assoc.
Ms. Tracy Orem, Exec. Dir.
Post Office Box 270
Webb City, MO 64876
Phone:314-636-8994
or
Mary Jane Landreth
5354 Foxfire
Joplin, MO 64804
or
Mrs. Jayne Watson
13 Brook Mill Lane
Chesterfield, MO 63017
314-434-2074
or
Susan Sagarra
12615 Woodygrove Court
Creve Coeur, MO 63146
(314) 878-8059
or
Course Rating:
Sue Herndon
15509 W. 89th St.
Lenexa, KS 66217

US WOMENS GOLF ASSOCIATIONS BY STATE

MISSOURI (cont.)

Metropolitan Amateur Golf Assoc.
Mr. Tom O'Toole, Jr.
2900 S. Brentwood Blvd.
St. Louis, MO 63144
314-961-3300
FAX: 314-961-4425

Midwest Section Pga Of America
Jon Jacobson, Executive Director
1960 Copper Oaks Circle
Blue Springs, MO 64015
Tel: (816) 229-6565
Fax: (816) 229-9644

Missouri Sr. Women's Golf Association
Mrs. Virginia Parshall, Executive Sec.
3903 Woodrail On The Green
Columbia, MO 65203
Tel: (573) 449-6338

St. Louis Professional Business Women's Golf Association
Sally Faith
200 S. Hanley, Suite 500
St. Louis, MO 63105
(314) 746-9133

MONTANA

Montana State Women's Golf Association
Mrs. Sonja Dehn, Executive Secretary
1016 Carlos Drive
Great Falls, MT 59404
406-761-0868

NEBRASKA

Nebraska Women's Golf Assoc.
Ms. Therse Wanek, President
707 East 4th Street
McCook NE 69001
Phone:402-435-6573
Fax:402-435-1134

Nebraska Women's Amateur Golf Association
Kathy Wood
501 Road East 120
Ogallala, NE 69153
(308) 284-4275
nebwaga@usga.org

NEVADA

Northern Nevada Women's Golf Association
Mrs. Pat Combs
1995 Parkway Drive
Reno, NV 89502
or
Ms. Sandy Osborne
886 Marsh Avenue
Reno, NV 89509
702-786-1869

Women's Southern Nevada Golf Association
Mrs. Sherry Corsello
2275 Buckingham Court
Henderson, NV 89014
or
Ms. Susie Bullard, President
2845 Carmel Ridge Drive
Las Vegas, NV 89134
702-228-9930

US WOMENS GOLF ASSOCIATIONS BY STATE

NEW HAMPSHIRE

New Hampshire Women's Golf Association
Pat Jewell
15 Lisa Beth Circle
Dover, NH 03820
Tel: 603-742-5540
or
Ms. Patti Wildman
7 Canary Lane
Bedford, NH 03110
603-472-5885

SWING
Sporting Women's Invitational Golf
Nancy Rollins, President
24 Barrett Road
New London, NH 03257
603-526-8619

NEW JERSEY

Women's New Jersey Golf Association
Ellen Gilbertson
16 North Ward Ave
Rumson, NJ 07760
or
Mrs. Ginnie Dillon
P.O. Box 537
Far Hills, NJ 07931
908-781-2774

South Jersey Golf Association
Arlene Cherwien
336 Highland Ave.
Vineland, NJ 08360
609-691-3737
Fax:609-507-1414
Email:sjga@usga.org
or
Nancy E. Lauber
144 Valley Forge Drive
Tuckerton, NJ 08087
609-296-5048

NEW MEXICO

Sun Country Amateur Golf Assoc.
Mr. J. P. Messick
10035 Country Club Lane NW, Suite 5
Albuquerque, NM 87114
505-897-0864
FAX: 505-897-3494

NEW YORK

Women's Metropolitan Golf Assoc.
Mrs. Dot Paluck
23 Flintlock Ct.
Bernardsville, NJ 07924
or
Mrs. Valerie Lazar
36 Seville Avenue
Rye, NY 10580
914-921-3392

Women's Buffalo District Golf Association
Ms. Ann Marie Luhr
234 Doncaster Road
Buffalo, NY 14217
716-875-6723
or
Mrs. Desanne Blaney
2490 West Oakfield Road
Grand Island, NY 14072
716-773-4562

Northeastern Women's Golf Association
Mrs. Susan Charbonneau
18 Deer Run
Gansevoort, NY 12831
or
Mrs. Diane Coughlin
1 Box 10A1
Stuyvesant, NY 12173
518-758-2483

US WOMENS GOLF ASSOCIATIONS BY STATE

NEW YORK (cont.)

**Syracuse Women's District
Golf Association**
Mrs. Toni Ann Tropea, President
5864 Highcrest Circle
East Syracuse, NY 13507
or
Ms. Nancy Rogers
7952 Lewis Lane
Fayetteville, NY 13066
315-637-6873
or
Course Rating:
Mrs. Bev Keyes
4249 Lucan Road
Liverpool, NY 13090
315-652-5657

**Women's Rochester District
Golf Association**
Mrs. Dolores Stieper
281 Bellmeade Road
Rochester, NY 14617
716-544-5865
or
Mrs. Tanya Durni
8 Bradford Hills Road
Fairfort, NY 14450
716-223-6962
or
Course Rating:
Mrs. Shirley Durham
880 Penfield Road
Rochester, NY 14625
716-381-1135

Utica Women's District Golf Assoc.
Mrs. Jane Eaton, President
Box 448
Norwich, NY 13815
607-334-9163

NORTH CAROLINA

**Women's Carolinas Golf Association
(NC AND SC)**
Mrs. Susan Harden, President
420 Wildwood Dunes Trail
Myrtle Beach, SC 29572
803-449-3005

**North Carolina Women's
Golf Association**
Mrs. Bobbie Burgess
Box 1613
Pinehurst, NC 28374
910-295-3000
sorvari@webster.campbell.edu
or
Mrs. Vicky DeSantis
1600 Morganton Road, Lot N-6
Pinehurst   NC   28374
Phone:910-692-8020

**Old North State Golf Association
(NC Senior Women)**
Ms. Jean Kirkman
28433 Forestdale Drive
Burlington, NC 27215
910-584-7125

NORTH DAKOTA

No listing

US WOMENS GOLF ASSOCIATIONS BY STATE

OHIO

**Women's Akron District
Golf Association**
Renee Jose
2232 Lancaster Rd
Akron, OH 44313
or
Mrs. Jane Ann Mougey
230 College Street
Hudson, OH 44236
216-650-0428

**Greater Cincinnati Women's
Golf Association**
Mrs. Mary Hackman
10010 Windzag Lane
Cincinnati, OH 45242
or
Mrs. Elaine Lazarus
3024 Burning Tree Lane
Cincinnati, OH 45237
513-351-0400

**Columbus Women's District
Golf Association**
Mrs. Betsey Mitchell
7270 Duncans Drive
Westerville, OH 43082
or
Mrs. Jeanne Rothe
2138 Sheringham Road
Columbus, OH 43220
614-451-9994

Dayton District Women's Golf Assoc.
Diana L. Schwab, President
4813 Rean Meadow
Kettering, OH 45440-2030
513-435-9311
or
Course Rating:
Sue Seitz
1115 Birchton Place
Vandalia, OH 45377

OHIO (cont.)

**Toledo Women's District
Golf Association**
Mrs. Vicki Nissen, Exec. Dir.
2530 Gleneagle Road
Perrysburg OH 43551
Phone:419-476-3633

**Cleveland Women's
Golf Association**
Mrs. Patty Jacobson, President
2631 Lander Road
Pepper Pike, OH 44124
or
Mrs. Maria Walzer
3365 Ardmore Road
Shaker Heights, OH 44120
216-561-2298
or
Course Rating:
Kathleen Newton
37620 Harlow Drive
Willoughby, OH 44094

OKLAHOMA

Women's Oklahoma Golf Assoc.
Mrs. Pat McKamey, President
10215 South Knoxville
Tulsa, OK 74137
918-299-3328
or
Ms. Sharon Garner
846 Lynwood Lane
Broken Arrow, OK 74011
918-455-7965

OREGON - No listing

US WOMENS GOLF ASSOCIATIONS BY STATE

PENNSYLVANIA

Women's Golf Assoc. of Philadelphia
Miss Charlotte N. Barnhard
Mailing address:
Drawer 808
Southeastern, PA 19399-0808
Street address:
700 Croton Road
Wayne, PA 19087
610-687-2340
Fax: 610-687-2082

**Women's Golf
Association of Western Pennsylvania**
Mrs. Susan Austin, Executive Secretary
6 Parkridge Lane
Pittsburgh, PA 15228-1106
412-341-0505
FAX: 412-341-6612

**Women's Central Pennsylvania
Golf Association**
Ms. Pat Wallace, President
2130 North 17th Street
Reading, PA 19604
or
Ms. Barbara Mader
2 Oak Place
Bernville, PA 19506
610-488-7299

Keystone Public Golf Association
Ms. Lois Sparrow
Mailing address:
P.O. Box 399
Export, PA 15632
Street address:
2186 Locust Street
Export, PA 15632
412-468-8850
FAX: 412-468-8897

RHODE ISLAND

Rhode Island Women's Golf Assoc.
Mrs. Susan Musche
284 Pleasant Street
Rumford, RI 02916
or
Mrs. Jerry Sansiveri
40 Pinewood Drive
North Providence, RI 02904
401-353-1025

**SWING
Sporting Women's Invitational Golf**
Lynn Schifino
P.O. Box 15424
Riverside, RI 02915

SOUTH CAROLINA

**Women's Carolinas Golf Association
(NC AND SC)**
Mrs. Susan Harden, President
420 Wildwood Dunes Trail
Myrtle Beach, SC 29572
803-449-3005

**Women's South Carolina
Golf Association**
Ms. Inez Long, Executive Secretary
P. O. Box 1745
Bluffton, SC 29910
803-757-4653
or
Course Rating:
Jean Pennington
1003 Sunset Drive
Mauldin, SC 29662

SOUTH DAKOTA - No listing

US WOMENS GOLF ASSOCIATIONS BY STATE

TENNESSEE

Women's Tennessee Golf Assoc.
Tina Sanders
12212 Oakmont Circle
Knoxville, TN 37922
423-966-3331
or
Mrs. Mary Watkins
1102 Woodward Avenue
Athens, TN 37303
615-745-3103

Chattanooga Women's Golf Assoc.
Mrs. Betty Robinson
8037 Savannah Trail
Ooltewah, TN 37363
or
Mrs. Kathy Wilkerson
2113 Ashley Lane
Hixson, TN 37343
615-843-0206

TEXAS

Women's Texas Golf Association
Rebecca Spears
619 Hillsong
San Antonio, TX 78258
or
Carolyn Henry, President
109 Top O'The Lake
Austin, TX 78734
512-261-8707

UTAH

Utah State's Women's Golf Association
Linda K. Olsen, President
3088 So. Sunset Hollow Dr.
Bountiful, Utah 84010
801-292-1674

VERMONT

Vermont State Women's Golf Assoc.
Ms. Sally Guerette
33 Mountainview Boulevard
South Burling, VT 05403
802-862-7161
or
Mrs. Kathy Allbright
P. O. Box 272
Meriden, NH 03770
603-469-3487
or
Course Rating:
Mrs. Pat Job
Sunset Drive
RR #2, Box 8853
Rutland, VT 05701
802-775-2743

VIRGINIA

Virginia State Golf Association Women's Division
Dr. Ruth Ann Verell
6215 Thornwood Drive
Alexandria, VA 22310
or
Mrs. Barbara Fleming
700 Oriole Drive #8414
Virginia Beach, VA 23451
804-428-5986
or
Ms. Meg Gilmore
301 C Second Street Northwest
Charlottesville VA 22902

Tournament Golf Association of Virginia
7892 Virginia Oaks Drive
Gainseville, VA 20155-2835
800-929-7449 (FAX: 703-754-8285)
info@virginiatga.com

US WOMENS GOLF ASSOCIATIONS BY STATE

WASHINGTON
No listing

WEST VIRGINIA
No listing

WISCONSIN
No listing

WYOMING

**Women's Wyoming State
Golf Association**
Ms. Diana Johnson, Exec. Sec.
1808 Kit Carson
Casper, WY 82604
307-265-8445
Fax: 307-265-0668

INTERNATIONAL JUNIOR GOLF ASSOCIATIONS

International Jr. Golf Assoc.
Ray Travagloine
803-785-4540
Golf Academy of Hilton Head
1519 Main Street Village
Hilton Head, SC 2926

International Junior Golf Tour
Vern Ford
800-494-4548
222 West Comstock Ave Suite 208
Winter Park, FL 32789

British Columbia Jr. Golf
Bernie Monteleone
604-765-1407
650 Dodd Road, Rutland School
Kelowna, BC V1X2X3

Royal Academy of Golf
Earl Fritz
416-674-0218
57 Galaxy Blvd., Suite 9
Etobicoke Ontario, Canada M9W5P1

MAJOR U.S. JUNIOR NATIONAL ASSOCIATIONS

Junior Golf Council
407-351-4653
P. O. Box 452
Winter Park, FL 32790

PGA Foundation
Steve Jubb
407-624-8498
100 Avenue of the Champions
Palm Beach Gardens, FL 33418

USGA For Juniors
Tom Meeks
908-234-2300
Golf House
P. O. Box 708
Far Hills, NJ 07931-0708

U.S. Challenge Cup Foundation
Dave Adominis, Jr.
401-301-4653

AJGA
Chris Haack
404-998-4653
2415 Steeplechase Lane
Roswell, GA 30076-3579

National Association of Junior Golfers
Tom Griffin
207-935-7080
21 Portland Street
Fryburg, ME 04037

National Junior Golf Assoc.
Jack Walsh
412-361-5014
6924 Bishop St.
Pittsburgh, PA 15206

JUNIOR GOLF ASSOCIATIONS BY STATE

ALABAMA

Alabama Jr. Golf Assoc.
Buford McCarthy
205-979-1234
1025 Montgomery Hwy., St 210
Birmingham, AL 35216

Dixie PGA
B. G. Simmons
205-991-8610
Inverness CC, Box 43248
Birmingham, AL 35243

ARIZONA

Arizona Jr. Golf Assoc.
Tom Cunningham
602-944-3035
7226 N. 16th Street, St 200
Phoenix, AZ 85020

Jr. Golf Association of Arizona
Tom Cunningham
602-944-6168
2116 West Peoria Avenue, Suite 1
Phoenix, AZ 85029

LPGA Girls Golf Club
Sandy La Bauve
602-451-8087
c/o Stonecreek Golf Club
12703 E. Altadena Ave.
Scottsdale, AZ 85259

ARKANSAS

Arkansas State Jr. Golf Assoc.
Bobbie O'Quin
501-227-8555
2311 Biscayne, St 206
Little Rock, AR 72227

COLORADO

Aspen Junior Golf Foundation
Doug Rohrbaugh
970-920-3221
P.O. Box 3273
Aspen, CO 81612

Colorado Jr. Golf
Doug Phelps
303-779-4653
5655 S. Yosemite, St 101
Englewood, CO 80111

Colorado Section PGA
Myran Craig
303-745-3697
12323 East Cornwel, St 212
Aurora, CO 80014

Grandjunction Jr. Golf
Jacque Gaskill
303-242-8842
2310 Cypress Ct.
Grand Junction, CO 81506

CALIFORNIA

AT&T Pebble Beach Jr. Golf
Sharon Pelino
408-375-0155
P. O. Box 4548
Carmel, CA 93921

Desert Jr. Golf Assoc.
Holly Neal
619-776-5777
41945 Boardwalk, St G
Palm Desert, CA 92211

Northern California Section PGA
Brian Baylis
510-455-7800
2133 Las Positas Court, Suite A
Livermore, CA 94550-9774

JUNIOR GOLF ASSOCIATIONS BY STATE

CALIFORNIA (cont.)

North California Jr. Golf
Sally Pini
408-425-0367
114 Arroyo Ct
Santa Cruz, CA 95060

Sacramento Area Youth Golf
Pat Campbell
916-429-0422
2 Pebble Court
Sacramento, CA 95831

San Diego Jr. Golf
Ralph Dittenhoefer
619-280-8505
3333 Camino del Rio South, #100
San Diego, CA 92108

Santa Barbara Junior Golf
Wade T. Nomura
805-684-4380
5410 Hales Lane
Carpenteria, CA 93013

Southern Cal PGA
Kevin Ostroske
714-776-4653
601 S. Valencia, St 200
Brea, CA 92621

Temecula Valley Jr. Golf
Tom Williams
909-677-7446
38275 Murrieta Hot Springs Rd.
Murrieta, CA 92563

CONNECTICUT
Connecticut State Golf/PGA
Tom Hantke
203-257-4653
35 Cold Spring Road, St 212
Rocky Hill, CT 06067

FLORIDA

Greater Tampa Jr. Golf
Mike Shumaker
407-823-1465
University of Cent. Florida
1020 Nancy Circle
Winter Springs, FL 32708

International Junior Golf Tour
Vern Ford
800-494-4548
222 West Comstock Ave Suite 208
Winter Park, FL 32789

LPGA
Betsy Clark
904-254-8800
2570 W. International Speedway Blvd
Suite B
Daytona Beach, FL 32114

LPGA Junior Girls Golf Club
904-254-8800
2570 Volusia Ave, St B
Daytona Beach, FL 32114

Junior Golf Council
407-351-4653
P. O. Box 452
Winter Park, FL 32790

Northern Florida PGA
Jerry Porter
904-322-0899
200 Forest lake Blvd.,St 3
Daytona Beach, FL 32119

PGA Foundation
Steve Jubb
407-624-8498
100 Avenue of the Champions
Palm Beach Gardens, FL 33418

JUNIOR GOLF ASSOCIATIONS BY STATE

FLORIDA (cont.)

South Florida Section PGA
Christie Dale
305-752-9299
10804 W. Sample Road
Coral Springs, FL 33065

Southwest Florida Jr. Golf
Jean Rubideaux
941-267-3332
P.O. Box 214
Estero, FL 33928-0214

Southwest Florida Junior Golf
Brian Fritz
813-542-5336
P.O. Box 1425
Cape Coral, FL 33910

U. S. Golf Alliance
Frank Ciarlo
904-893-2991
4134 Chelmsford Road
Tallahasse, FL 32308

GEORGIA

Atlanta Jr. Golf
Merilee Giddings
404-850-9040
121 Village Parkway, Bldg 3
Murrietta, GA 3067

Georgia Section PGA
Peter Ripa
404-952-9063
1165 Northchase Parkway, St 230
Marietta, GA 30067

GEORGIA (cont.)

Southeastern Junior Golf Tour
Todd Thompson
770-664-1444
465 Mikasa Dr.
Alpharetta, GA 30202

AJGA
Chris Haack
404-998-4653
2415 Steeplechase Lane
Roswell, GA 30076-3579

HAWAII

Aloha Section PGA
Richie Okamura
808-875-5111
Wailea Golf Club
100 Wailea Golf Club Drive
Kihei, HI 96753

IDAHO

Idaho Jr. Golf Assoc.
Vicky Davis
208-342-4442
P. O. Box 3025
Boise, ID 83703

Rocky Mountain PGA
Susan Breaux
208-939-6028
595 E. State St.
Eagle, ID 83616

JUNIOR GOLF ASSOCIATIONS BY STATE

ILLINOIS

Illinois Jr. Golf Assoc.
Roger Ulseth
708-257-9806
1 Pete Dye Drive
Lemont, IL 60439

Illinois Section PGA
Mike Miller
708-257-9600
1 Pete Dye Drive
Lemont, IL 60439

INDIANA

Indiana Junior Golf Assoc.
R. E. Buffy Mayerstein
317-447-1992
P. O. Box 4454
Lafayette, IN 47903

Indiana PGA
Trent Hicks
317-738-9696
P. O. Box 516
Franklin, IN 46131

Evansville IN Jr. Golf
Dean Brinker
812-476-0651
111 S. Greenriver Road
Evansville, IN 47715

Fort Wayne IN Jr. Golf
Milt Eley
219-489-6421
705 E. State Blvd.
Fort Wayne, IN 46805

IOWA

Iowa Section PGA
Blake Dodge
319-378-9142
1930 St. Andrews N.E.
Cedar Rapids, IA 52402

KENTUCKY

Kentucky Golf Assoc & PGA Sec.
Brandon Neal
502-499-7255
P. O. Box 18396
Louisville, KY 40261

LOUISIANA

Gulf States Section PGA
Dick Walcott
504-245-7333
P. O. Box 29426
New Orleans, LA 70189

JUNIOR GOLF ASSOCIATIONS BY STATE

MAINE

Maine State Golf Assoc.
Ralph Noe
207-795-6742
P. O. Box 419
Auburn, ME 04212

National Assoc. of Junior Golfers
Tom Griffin
207-935-7080
21 Portland Street
Fryburg, ME 04037

MARYLAND

Mid-Atlantic PGA
Ken Kuhn
301-621-8320
2721 Jefferson Davis Hwy Suite 101
Stafford, MD 22554

MASSACHUSETTS

Massachusetts Golf Assoc.
Tom Landry
617-449-3000
175 Highland Avenue
Needham, MA 02192

New England PGA
Ed Carbone
617-246-4653
1 Audobon Road
Wakefield, MA 01880

MICHIGAN

Flint Junior Golf Association
Bob Bernstein
810-694-0906
11422 Woodbridge
Grand Blanc, MI 48439

Michigan Section PGA
Ron Burchi
313-522-2323
32744 Five Mile Road
Livonia, MI 48154

Power-Bilt PGA Junior Tour
Rolla Frisinger
517-278-4892
42 Narrows Rd.
Coldwater, MI 49036

The Junior Tour
Hank Andries
313-642-6120
3904 West Maple Road, #300
Bloomfield Hills, MI 48301-3220

U. S. High School Golf Assoc.
Hank Andries
810-540-7555
3904 West Maple Road, Suite 300
Bloomfield Hills, MI 48301

JUNIOR GOLF ASSOCIATIONS BY STATE

MINNESOTA

Minnesota Section PGA
John & Tracy Johnson
612-754-0820
Bunker Hills CC
Highway 242 & Foley Blvd.
Coon Rapids, MN 55448

MISSOURI

Missouri Golf Assoc.
Bill Wells
314-636-8994
P. O. Box 104164
1808 B Southwest Blvd.
Jefferson City, MO 65109

Midwest Section PGA
Steve Specht
816-229-6565
P.O. Box 553
Blue Springs, MO 64013

Gateway PGA
Shannon Miller
314-991-4994
12225 Clayton Road
St. Louis, MO 63131

NEBRASKA

Nebraska Section PGA
Bruce Lubach
402-489-7760
9301 Firethorn Lane
Lincoln, NE 68520

NEVADA

**Southern Nevada
Junior Golf Association**
Jane Schlosser
702-433-0626
3430 E. Flamingo Rd. # 244
Las Vegas, NV 89121

Northern Nevada Jr. Golf
John & Pam Whalen
702-673-4653
P. O. Box 5630
Sparks, NV 89432

NEW HAMPSHIRE

New Hampshire Golf Association
Bruce Syphers
603-436-8117
7 Fairway Drive
Greenland, NH 03840

NEW JERSEY

New Jersey PGA
Walter Syring
908-521-4000
P. O. Box 200
1 Forsgate Drive
Jamesburg, NJ 0831

JUNIOR GOLF ASSOCIATIONS BY STATE

NEW MEXICO

Sun Country Section PGA
John Speary
505-271-1442
Mountain Run Center
5850 Eubank NE, Suite B-72
Albuquerque, NM 87111

NEW YORK

Buffalo District Golf Assoc.
Whitey Nichols
716-632-1936
P.O. Box 19
Cheektowaga, NY 14225

Northeastern NY PGA
Bill Melchionni
518-463-3067
48 Howard Street
Albany, NY 12207

Central NY PGA
Ron Stepanek
315-468-6812
822 State Fair Blvd.
Syracuse, NY 13209

Metropolitan PGA
Bill McMannis
914-347-2416
49 Knollwood Road, St 200
Elmsford, NY 10523

Metropolitan Golf Association
Bill McCarthy
914-347-4653
125 Spencer Pl., Box 219
Mamaroneck, NY 10543

NEW YORK (cont.)

Rochester District Golf Assoc.
Brian Ward
716-292-5950
333 Metro Park
Rochester, NY 14623

Syracuse District Golf Assoc.
Al Highducheck
315-445-1893
243 Marsh Drive
Dewitt, NY 13214

Western NY PGA
Bill Dimas
716-626-0603
P. O. Box 1728
Williamsville, NY 14231-1728

NORTH CAROLINA

Carolinas Golf Association
Darrell Tubner
910-673-1000
P. O. Box 319
West End, NC 27376

JUNIOR GOLF ASSOCIATIONS BY STATE

OHIO

Northern Ohio PGA
Sue Davies
216-951-4546
38121 Euclid Avenue
Willoughby, OH 44094

Miami Valley Ohio Jr. Golf
Gary Goecke
513-372-7437
944 Country Club Drive
Xenia, OH 45385

Southern Ohio PGA
Laura Alger
614-221-7194
17 S. High Street, St 1200
Columbus, OH 43215

OKLAHOMA

Oklahoma Golf Association
Rick Coe
405-848-0042
6217 N. Classen Blvd.
Oklahoma City, OK 73116

South Central PGA Jr. Assoc.
Walter Hopper
918-825-3056
Pryor Golf Course, HCR 65
Box 115
Pryor, OK 74361

OREGON

Oregon Jr. Golf Fund
Charlotte Plank
503-643-2610
8364 SW Nimbus
Beaverton, OR 97005

PENNSYLVANIA

National Junior Golf Assoc.
Jack Walsh
412-361-5014
6924 Bishop St.
Pittsburgh, PA 15206

Western PA Golf Assoc.
Karen
412-963-9806
1360 Old Freeport Road, St 1BR
Pittsburgh, PA 15238

Tri-State Section PGA
Dennis Darak
412-774-2224
221 Sherwood Srive
Monaca, PA 15061

Philadelphia Section PGA
JoAnn Fisher
610-277-5777
Plymouth Green Office Campus
801 E. Germantown Pike #F-6
Norristown, PA 19401

RHODE ISLAND

Rhode Island Golf
Dave Adamonis
401-421-4653
1664 Hartford Ave., St 32
Johnston, RI 02919

U.S. Challenge Cup Foundation
Dave Adominis, Jr.
401-301-4653
Johnston, RI

JUNIOR GOLF ASSOCIATIONS BY STATE

SOUTH CAROLINA

Carolina's PGA
Darrell Bock
803-399-2742
3852 HWY 9 East
N. Myrtle Beach, SC 29597

International Jr. Golf Assoc.
Ray Travagloine
803-785-4540
Golf Academy of Hilton Head
1519 Main Street Village
Hilton Head, SC 2926

TENNESSEE

Tennessee Section PGA
Allen Richardson
615-790-7600
400 Franklin Road
Franklin, TN 37069

Knoxville Area Junior Golf Association
Reid Harris
615-966-9103
P.O. Box 10409
Knoxville, TN
37939-0409

TEXAS

Southern Texas PGA
David Findlay
713-363-0511
1776 Woodstead Ct., St 220
The Woodlands, TX 77380

TEXAS (cont.)

Houston Golf Association
Julie Robichaux
713-367-7999
1830 South Millbend Dr.
The Woodlands, TX 77380

North Texas PGA
Rich Richardson
214-881-4653
500 No. Central Expressway, St 272
Plaon, TX 75074

UTAH

Utah Section PGA
Jeff Thurman
801-532-7421
419 E. 100th South
Salt Lake City, UT 84111

VERMONT

Vermont Golf Assoc.
Jim Bassett
802-773-7180
P.O. Box 1612 Station A
Rutland, VT 05701

WASHINGTON

Washington Jr. Golf Assoc.
Joan Teats
206-564-0348
633 N. Mildred, St C
Tacoma, WA 98406-1725

JUNIOR GOLF ASSOCIATIONS BY STATE

VIRGINIA

Virginia State Golf Assoc.
Thomas W. Smith
804-378-2300
830 Southlake Blvd., St A
Richmond, VA 23236

Jr. Golfers of Washington D.C.
Bob Riley
703-569-6311
8012 Colorado Springs Drive
Springfield, VA 22153-2721

IIAJC
Jill Kriser
800-221-7917
127 S. Peyton Street
Alexandria, VA 22314-2830

WASHINGTON

Pacific Northwest Section PGA
Mark Lynch
360-456-6496
4011 Yelm Highway SE
Olympia, WA 98501-5170

WISCONSIN

Wisconsin Section PGA
Joe Stradler
414-365-4474
4000 W. Brown Deer Road
Milwaukee, WI 53209

WISCONSIN (cont.)

Wisconsin State Golf
Gene Haas
414-786-4301
333 Bishops Way
Brookfield, WI 53005

Golf Foundation of Wisconsin
Carl Unis
414-365-4471
4000 West Brown Dear Rd.
Milwaukee, WI 53209

MAJOR INTERNATIONAL GOLF ASSOCIATIONS:

U.S.G.A.
World Amateur Golf Council
Golf House
P.O. Box 708
Far Hills, NJ 07931-0708
Tel. 908-234-2300
Fax 908-234-2178

Canadian Ladies' Golf Association
Peggy Brown
National Executive Director
Golf House, Glen Abbey Golf Club
1333 Dorval Drive
Oakville, Ontario L6J 4Z3
Tel: (905) 849-CLGA ext. 24
1-800-455-CLGA
Fax: (905) 849-0188

Royal Canadian Golf Association
1333 Dorval Dr.
Oakville, Ontario
L6J 4Z3 Canada
Phone: 416-844-1800

The Canadian Professional
Golfers' Association
R.R. #1, 13450 Dublin Line
Acton, Ontario
L7J 2W7
Telephone: (519) 853-5450
Fax: (519) 853-5449
E-mail: cpga@CanadianPGA.org

R&A
Royal and Ancient
Golf Club of St. Andrews
St. Andrews,
Fife KY16 9JD
Scotland
Tel.: 011-441-334-472112
Fax: 011-441-334-477580

European Golf Association
Place de la Croix-Blanche 19
P.O. Box CH – 1066
 Epalinges, Switzerland
Tel.: 41-21-784 35 32
Fax: 41-21-784 3536

Pga European Tour
European Senior Tour
European Challenge Tour
Wentworth Club
Wentworth Drive
Virginia Water
Surrey, GU25 4LS
England
Tel.: 011- 441-344-842-881

INTERNATIONAL GOLF ASSOCIATIONS BY COUNTRY

ALGERIA

Federation Algerienne de Golf
Rue Ahmed OUAKED
Dely-Ibrahim, Algeria
Phone: 213-278-1733
Fax: 213-261-4133

ARGENTINA

Asociacion Argentina de Golf
Corrientes 538 - pisos 11 y 12
(1043) Buenos Aires, Argentina
Phone: 541-325-7498
Fax: 541-325-8660

AUSTRALIA

Australian Golf Union
Golf Australia House
155 Cecil Street
South Melbourne,
Victoria 3205, Australia
Phone: 613 3699-7944
Fax: 613 3690-8510

NSW Golf Association A.C.N.
17 Brisbane Street
Darlinghurst NSW 2010
P O Box 704,
Darlinghurst NSW 1300
Tel: 61 2 9264 8433
Fax: 61 2 9261 4750
nswga@nswga.com.au

Queensland Golf Union
Cnr Wren Street and Walden Lane
Bowen Hills QLD 4006
GPO BOX 1518, Brisbane QLD 4001
Tel (07) 3854 1105
Fax (07) 3257 1520

AUSTRALIA (cont.)

Tasmanian Golf Council Inc
2 Queen Street, Bellerive,
Tasmania 7018
PO Box 410 Rosny Park,
Tasmania 7018
Tel: (03) 62 44 3600
Fax: (03) 62 44 3201

Victorian Golf Association
The Victorian Golf Association
PO Box 187, Burwood VIC 3125
Tel: (03) 9889 6731
Fax: (03) 9889 1077

The Western Australian Golf Assoc.
Suite 1-5, 49 Melville Parade,
South Perth WA 6151
P O Box 455, South Perth 6951
Tel: (08) 9367 2490
Fax: (08) 9368 2255

South Australian Golf Assoc.
The South Australian Golf Assoc.
PO Box 356,
Torrensville Plaza SA 5031
Tel: (08) 8352 6899
Fax: (08) 8350 3900

**PGA - Australian
Professional Golfers' Association**
113 Queen Street
Strathfield, New South Wales, 2137
Australia

AUSTRIA

Osterreichischer Golf-Verband
Haus des Sports
Prinz-Eugen-Strasse 12
A-1040 Wien, Austria
Phone: 43-222-505-3245
Fax: 43-222-505-4962

INTERNATIONAL GOLF ASSOCIATIONS BY COUNTRY

BAHAMAS

Bahamas Golf Federation
P.O. Box F-42203
Freeport, Bahamas
Phone: 809-328-8943
Fax: 809-323-8719

BELGIUM

Royal Belgian Golf Federation
Mr. Christian Moyson
Deputy General Secretary
Chaussee de la Hulpe, 110
1050 Brussels
Tel: 32 2 672 23 89
Fax: 32 2 672 08 97

Federation Royale Belge de Golf
Chaussee de la Hulpe, 110
1050 Brussels, Belgium
Phone: 322-672-2389
Fax: 322-672-0897

BERMUDA
Bermuda Golf Association
P.O. Box HM 433
Hamilton HM BX, Bermuda
Phone: 809-238-1367
Fax: 809-238-0983

BOTSWANA

Botswana Golf Union
P.O. Box 1033
Gaborone, Botswana

BRAZIL

Confederacao Brasileira de Golfe
Rua 7 de Abril, 282-8°
ANDAR-SALA 83
01044 Sao Paulo, Brazil
Phone: 011-259-7511
Fax: 0055011-259-7861

BURMA

Burma Golf Federation
c/o Aung San Stadium
Rangoon, Burma

CANADA

Royal Canadian Golf Association
Golf House
1333 Dorval Drive, R.R. #2
Oakville, Ontario L6J, Canada
Phone: 905-844-1800
Fax: 905-845-7040

Canadian Ladies' Golf Association
Ms. Midge Prong
R.R. #1 Lisle
Ontario, Canada L0M 1M0
705-435-3130

CAYMAN ISLANDS

Cayman Islands Golf Association
c/o Cayman National Trust Company
P.O. Box 1790 G
Grand Cayman, Cayman Islands

INTERNATIONAL GOLF ASSOCIATIONS BY COUNTRY

CHILE

Federacion Chilena de Golf
California 1945, Depto. F
Casilla 49, Correo 29
Santiago, Chile
Phone: 562-204-8947
Fax: 562-225-7106

CHINA, REPUBLIC OF CHINA

GAROC
Golf Association of the
Republic of China
12th Floor
125, Nanking East Road, Section 2,
Taipei, Taiwan 104,
Republic of China
Phone: 886-2-516-5611
Fax: 886-2-516-3208

Mr. Frank C. F. Chang
Secretary General
71, Lane 369, Tunhua S. Road
Taipei, Taiwan (10647)
Republic of China
Tel: 886-2-711-3046
Fax: 886-2-777-4178

COLOMBIA

Colombian Golf Federation
Mr. Jorge A. Cabrera
Executive Director
Carrera 7a. No. 72-64
Santafe de Bogota
Colombia, SA

Federacion Colombiana de Golf
Carrera 7A, No. 72-64
Of. Int. 26, Apartado Aereo 90985
Bogota, D.E., Colombia

COOK ISLANDS

Rarotonga Golf Club, Inc.
c/o Les Win, Club Manager
P.O. Box 151
Rarotonga, Cook Islands
Phone: 682-27-360
Fax: 682-25-420

COSTA RICA

Asociacion Nacional de Golf
P.O. Box 10969
San Jose 1000, Costa Rica
Phone: 506-282-6447

CZECH REPUBLIC
Czech Golf Federation
Erpet Golf Center
Strakonicka 510
15000 Prague 5-Smichov,
Czech Republic
Phone: 422-544586

DENMARK

Danish Golf Union
Idraettens Hus
Brondby Stadion 20
DK-2605, Brondby, Denmark
Phone: 45-43-26-2700
Fax: 45-43-26-2701

Dansk Golf Union
Mr. Thorleik Nellemann
Fuglevaenget 55
DK-3520 Farum
Denmark
Tel: 4543262700
Fax: 4543262701

INTERNATIONAL GOLF ASSOCIATIONS BY COUNTRY

DOMINICAN REPUBLIC

Dominican Golf Association
Apartado 3584
Santo Domingo, Dominican Republic
Phone: 809-689-7737
Fax: 809-687-6474

ECUADOR

Federacion Ecuatoriana de Golf
P.O. Box 07-21-2411
Quito, Ecuador
Phone: 593-2-538726
Fax: 593-2-533809

EGYPT

The Egyptian Golf Federation
Gezira Sporting Club
Gezira, Cairo, Egypt

El Salvador

Asociacion Salvadorena de Golf
Apartado Postal 631
San Salvador, El Salvador
Phone: 503-31-2033
Fax: 503-31-2234

ENGLAND

Professional Golfers Association
PGA Britain
Apollo House
The Belfry, Sutton Coldfield
West Midlands, England B76 9TP
(0675)470333

PGA European Tour
Wentworth Drive
Virginia Water
Surrey, England GU254LX
044 842 881

ENGLAND (cont.)

English Golf Union
The National Golf Centre
Woodhall Spa
Lincolnshire, England LN10 6PU
Tel: 44 [0] 1526 354500
Fax: 44 [0] 1526 354020

Golf Foundation
Foundation House
Hanbury Manor
Ware, Hertfordshire SG12 0UH
England
Tel: 44 [0] 1920 484044
Fax: 44 [0] 1920 484055

FIJI

Fiji Golf Association
G.P.O. Box 13843
Suva, Fiji
Phone: 679-313213
Fax: 679-301647

FINLAND

Finnish Golf Union
Mr. Osmo Saarinen
General Secretary
Radiokatu 20
PL 27, SF-00241 Helsinki
Finland
Tel: 358-0158-2244
Fax: 358-0147-145

Radiokatu 12
SF-00240 Helsinki, Finland
Phone: 358-0-158-2244
Fax: 358-0-147-145

INTERNATIONAL GOLF ASSOCIATIONS BY COUNTRY

FRANCE

Federation Francaise de Golf
69 Avenue Victor Hugo
75783 Paris, Cedex 16, France
Phone: 331-4502-1355
Fax: 331-4417-6363

GERMANY

Deutscher Golf Verband eV.
Postfach 21 06
Lederberg 25
6200 Wiesbaden, Germany
Phone: 49-6121-526041
Fax: 49-6121-599493

Deutscher Golf Verband e.V.
Dr. Wolfgang Scheuer
President
Postfach 21 06
65011 Wiesbaden
Germany
Tel: (06-11) 9 90 20-0
Fax: (06-11) 9 90 20-40

GREAT BRITAIN

Royal and Ancient
Golf Club of St. Andrews
Fife KY16 9JD, Scotland
Phone: 44-334-72112
Fax: 44-334-77580

GREECE

Hellenic Golf Federation
P.O. Box 70003
GR-166 10 Glyfada
Athens, Greece
Phone: 301-894-5727
Fax: 301-894-5162

GUATEMALA

Federacion Guatemalteca de Golf
3a Avenida Finca El Zapote
Zona 2 Guatemala, Guatemala

HONDURAS

Asociacion Hondurena de Golf
Apartado Postal No. 3175
Tegucigalpa, Honduras
Phone: 504-37-2084; 504-37-2480
Fax: 504-38-0456

HONG KONG

The Golf Association of Hong Kong
Mr. Allistair Polson
General Manager
Room 1420, Prince's Building
10, Chater Road
Hong Kong
Tel: (852) 5228804
Fax: (852) 8451553

Hong Kong Chinese Lady Golfers Assoc.
Ms. Agnes Ng
Hon. Secretary
38/F, Unit B
Bank of China Tower
No. 1 Garden Road
Hong Kong
Tel: (852) 869-6581
Fax: (852) 868-4642

HUNGARY

Hungarian Golf Federation
Dozsa Gyorgy-ut 1-3, H-1143
Budapest, Hungary
Phone: 361-113-6639
Fax: 361-113-6463

INTERNATIONAL GOLF ASSOCIATIONS BY COUNTRY

ICELAND

Golf Union of Iceland
Sport Center
P.O. Box 1076
121 Reykjavik, Iceland
Phone: 354-1-686686
Fax: 354-1-29520

Frimann Gunnlaugsson
Sport Center
104 Reykjavik
Iceland
Tel: 354-1-686686
Fax: 354-1-686086

INDIA

The Indian Golf Union
SUKH SAGAR (2nd floor)
2/5 Sarat Bose Road
Calcutta 700 200, India
Phone: 91-33-745795
Fax: 91-33-748914

INDONESIA
Indonesia Golf Association
JL Rawamangun Muka Raya
Jakarta 13220, Indonesia
Phone: 62-21-481208;
or 62-21-485298

ISRAEL

Israel Golf Federation
P.O. Box 1010
Caearea, Israel 30660
Phone: 972-636-1174
Fax: 972-636-1173

ITALY

Federazione Italiana Golf
Vaile Tiziano, 74
00196, Roma, Italy
Phone: 396-368-58108
Fax: 396-322-0250

Assgolf
Associazione Campi Pratica
Via Monte Cengio,
13 - 20138 Milano
Telephone 39-2-513311

Associazione Italiana Golfisti Seniores
Via Pontaccio 14
21121 Milano
Telephone 39-2-86462370
Fax: 8057531

Associazione Italiana Farmacisti Golfisti Farmagolf
Via Jappelli10
35121 Padova
Telephone: 39-49-875459

Associazione Golf Club Temi
C.so Magenta 43
20123 Milano
Telephone 39-2-48013071
Fax: 48008042

Associazione Italiana Segretari Di Golf E Green Keepers
C/o Golf Garlenda
Via del Golf 7
17030 Garlenda (SV)
Telephone 39-182-580012

Associazione Italiana Mid Amateurs
C/o Micron
Via E.Filiberto 4
20149 Milano
Telephone 39-2-33606730

INTERNATIONAL GOLF ASSOCIATIONS BY COUNTRY

ITALY (cont.)

**Associazione Italiana Architetti
Golfisti Archigolf**
c/o Golfacilities
Pizza Albania, 15 - 00153 Roma
Telephone 39-775-504545
Fax:505626

**Diplomatic And International
Golf Association**
Via G. Quattrucci, 117/B
00046 Grottaferrata (RM)
Telephone & Fax: 39-6-9410302

Italian Lady Association - L.g.a.
Editoriale Country & Sport
Via Mascagni 21
20122 Milano
Telephone 39-2-795600
Fax 795646

Pga Italiana
Via XX settembre,12
10121 Torino
Telefono (011) 5612018
Telefax (011) 5611996

Scuola Nazionale Di Golf
Centro tecnico Federale Italiano
Via di Monte Topino SS2
Cassia Km.44,500
Nepi Sutri (VT)
Tel. (0761) 600960
Telefax (0761)600791

IVORY COAST

Federation Nationale
Du Golf En Cote D'Ivoire
08 BP 1297
Abidjan 08,
Republique de Cote D'Ivoire
Phone: 225-213-874
Fax: 225-227-112

JAMAICA

Jamaica Golf Association
Constant Spring Golf Club
P.O. Box 743
Kingston 8, Jamaica
Phone: 809-925-2325
Fax: 809-924-6330

JAPAN

Japan Golf Association
606-6th Floor, Palace Building
Marunouchi, Chiyoda-ku
Tokyo, Japan
Phone: 813-215-0003
Fax: 813-214-2831

KOREA

Korea Golf Association
Room 1318, Manhattan Building
36-2, Yeo Eui Do-Dong,
Yeong Deung Po-Ku
Seoul, Korea
Phone: 822-783-4748
Fax: 822-783-4747

LATVIA

Latvia Golf Association
Drottninggatan 105 B,
S-252 33, Intl. Affa
Helsingborg, Sweden

INTERNATIONAL GOLF ASSOCIATIONS BY COUNTRY

LEBANON

Lebanese Golf Federation
c/o Mr. Mazzawi
Middle East Airlines
680 Fifth Avenue, Fifth Floor
New York, NY 10019
Phone: 212-478-1931

LIBYA

Libyan Golf Federation
P.O. Box 3674
Tripoli, Libya

LUXEMBOURG

Golf-Club Grand-Ducal de Luxembourg
1, route de Treves
2633 Senningerberg,
Grand Duchy of Luxembourg

MALAYSIA

Malaysian Golf Association
No. 12-A Persiaran Ampang
55000 Kuala Lumpur, Malaysia
Phone: 603-457-7931
Fax: 603-456-5596

MEXICO

Federacion Mexicana de Golf
A.C., Cincinati No. 40-104, Col. Napoles
03710 Mexico, D.F.
Phone: 525-543-3674

Federacion Mexicana De Golf, A.C.
Av. Lomas De Sotelo 1112, Desp. 103
Col. Lomas De Sotelo
Mexico D.F, Mexico C.P. 11200
Tel: (52-5) 395-32-45
Fax: (52-5) 580-22-63

MOROCCO

Federation Royale Marocaine de Golf
Royal Golf Rabat dar es Salam
Route des Zaers
Rabat, Morocco
Phone: 212-775-5636
Fax: 212-775-1026

NETHERLANDS

Nederlandse Golf Federatie
Soestdijkerstraatweg 172
1213 XJ Hilversum, Holland
Phone: 313-406-21888
Fax: 313-406-21177

Netherlands Golf Federation
Mr. Robert M. Hage
Rijnzathe 8
3458 PV De Meern
The Netherlands
Tel: 03406-21888

NEW ZEALAND

New Zealand Golf Association
Dominion Sports House
Victoria Street
P.O. Box 11842
Wellington, New Zealand
Phone: 644-472-2967
Fax: 644-472-7330

NICARAGUA

NAGA
Nicaraguan Golf Association
7413 S.W. 127th Place
Miami, FL 33183
U.S.A.
Phone: 305-441-7596
Fax: 305-385-1464

INTERNATIONAL GOLF ASSOCIATIONS BY COUNTRY

NIGERIA

Nigeria Golf Association
National Sports Commission
National Stadium Surulere
Lagos, Nigeria
Phone: 234-1-830649
Fax: 234-1-669444

NORWAY

Norges Golfforbund
Hauger Skolevei 1, 1351 Rud
Oslo, Norway
Phone: 47-287-4600

PAKISTAN

Pakistan Golf Federation
P.O. Box No. 1295
Rawalpindi, Pakistan
Phone: 92-51-372001
Fax: 92-51-379801

PANAMA

Panama Golf Association
P.O. Box 8613
Panama 5, Panama
Phone: 675-258-418

PAPUA NEW GUINEA

Papua New Guinea Golf Association
P.O. Box 4632
Boroko, Papua New Guinea
Phone: 675-323-1120
Fax: 675-323-1300

PARAGUAY

Asociacion Paraguaya de Golf
P.O. Box 1795
Asuncion, Paraguay
Phone: 595-21-36117
Fax: 595-21-595021

PERU

Federacion Peruana de Golf
Estadio Nacional
Puerto 4, Piso 4, Casilla 5637
Lima, Peru
Phone: 511-433-6515
Fax: 511-433-8267

PHILIPPINES

Philippines Golf Association
209 Administration Building
Rizal Memorial Sports Complex
Vito Cruz, Manila, Philippines
Phone: 632-588-845
Fax: 632-521-1587

PORTUGAL

Federacao Portuguesa de Golfe
Rua General Ferreira Martins, 10-5°
Miraflores, 1495 Algés, Portugal
Phone: 351-1-4107521
Fax: 351-1-4107972

PUERTO RICO
Puerto Rico Golf Association
G.P.O. Box 3862
San Juan, Puerto Rico 00936
Phone: 809-721-4918
Fax: 809-781-2210

INTERNATIONAL GOLF ASSOCIATIONS BY COUNTRY

QATAR

Qatar Golf Association
P.O. Box 6177
Doha, Qatar
Phone: 454284; 454287
Fax: 974-430132

RUSSIA

Russian Golf Association
18 Markhlevsky Street
Moscow, Russia

SAN MARINO

San Marino Golf Federation
Via XXV, Marzo 11
47031 Domagnano,
Republic of San Marino
Phone: 39-549-902508
Fax: 39-549-902516

SCOTLAND

Scottish Golf Union
Mr. Ian Hume, Secretary
The Cottage
181a Whitehouse Road
Edinburgh, Scotland
EH4 6By
Tel: 44-131-339-7546
Fax: 44-131-339-1169

Ladies' Golf Union
Mrs. Elaine A. Mackie
The Scores
St. Andrews
Fife, Scotland
KY16 9AT
Tel: 01334-475811
Fax: 01334-472818

SINGAPORE

Singapore Golf Association
Thomson Road
P.O. Box 0172
Singapore 9157
Phone: 65-764-0698
Fax: 65-765-8119

SOUTH AFRICA

South African Golf Federation
P.O. Box 391994
Bramley 2018
c/o Wanderers Club
Ielovo, Johannesburg, South Africa
Phone: 442-3723
Fax: 442-3753

SPAIN

Real Federacion Espanola de Golf
Capitan Haya, 9-5
28020 Madrid, Spain
Phone: 341-555-2682
Fax: 341-556-3290

SRI LANKA

Ceylon Golf Union
P.O. Box 309
Model Farm Road
Colombo 8, Sri Lanka

SWEDEN

Swedish Golf Federation
Box 84
S-182 11 Danderyd, Sweden
Phone: 468-662-1500
Fax: 468-755-8439

INTERNATIONAL GOLF ASSOCIATIONS BY COUNTRY

SWITZERLAND

Association Suisse de Golf
Mr. John C. Storjohann
General Secretary
Place de la Croix-Blanche 19
CH-1066 Epalingos
Switzerland
Tel: 021-784-3531
Fax: 021-784-3536

Association Suisse de Golf
En Ballegue, Case postale
CH-1066 Epalinges
Lausanne, Switzerland
Phone: 4121-784-3532
Fax: 4121-784-3536

THAILAND

Thailand Golf Association
1st Floor,
Petroleum Authority of Thailand Bld.
Bangkok 10900, Thailand
Phone: 662-537-8172
Fax: 662-537-8173

TRINIDAD & TOBAGO

Trinidad & Tobago Golf Association
P.O. Box 817
Newtown, Port of Spain, Trinidad
Phone: 809-622-2939
Fax: 809-622-7930

UNITED STATES

United States Golf Association
Golf House
P.O. Box 708
Far Hills, NJ 07931-0708, U.S.A.
Phone: 908-234-2300
Fax: 908-234-2178

UNITED STATES (cont.)

PGA
Professional Golf Asssociation
100 Avenue of the Champions
P.O. Box 109601
Palm Beach Gardens, Fla. 33410

LPGA Tour
2570 W. International Speedway B,
Suite B
Daytona Beach, Florida 32111-1118
Tel.: (904) 254-8800
WebSite:
http://www.lpga.com/tour/index.html
E-mail: info@lpga.com

Senior Pga Tour
112 TPC Boulevard
Ponte Vedra Beach, Florida 32082
Tel.: (904) 285-3700
WebSite: http://www.pgatour.com/

National Golf Association
1625 I St. N.W.
Washington, D.C. 20006
Phone: 202-625-2080

National Golf Foundation
1150 South U.S. Hwy. 1
Jupiter, Fla. 33477
Phone: 407-744-6006

American Junior Golf Association
2415 Steeplechase Lane
Roswell, Ga. 30076
Phone: 404-998-4653

PGA World Golf Hall of Fame
P.O. Box 1908
Pinehurst, N.C. 28374
Phone: 919-295-6651

Golf Writers Association of America
P.O. Box 328054
Farmington Hills, Mich. 48332
Phone: 313-442-1481

INTERNATIONAL GOLF ASSOCIATIONS BY COUNTRY

VANUATU

Vanuatu Golf Association
P.O. Box 309
Port Vila, Vanuatu
Tel. 678-24291

VENEZUELA

Federacion Venezolana de Golf
Unidad Comercial "La Florida"
Local 5, Avenida Avila, La Florida
Caracas 1050, Venezuela
Phone: 582-741-660
Fax: 582-742-731

Federacion Venezolana de Golf
Mr. Arnoldo Salazar, President
Unidad Commercial "La Florida"
Locales 6 y 7
Av. Avila
La Florida
Caracas, Venezuela 1050
Tel: 74.16.60   Fax: 74.27.31

ZIMBABWE

Zimbabwe Golf Association
P.O. Box 3327
Harare, Zimbabwe
Phone: 26-34-705-571
Fax: 26-34-732-445

U.S. GOLF MAGAZINES

Golf Course Living
NY Times Co. Magazine
5520 Park Ave.
Trumbull, CT. 06611-0395

Greensheet
P.O. Box 2287
Houston, TX. 77252-2287

Bottom Dollar Golf
2217 Lindell Ave.
Austin, TX. 78704

Golf Products News
11-15 River Rd.
Fairlawn, NJ. 07410

Golf And Travel
Columbus Circle Station
P.O Box 20466
New York, NY. 10023

The Counrty Club
16 Forrest Street
New Canaan, CT. 06840

Clubhouse
Focus On The Family
Colorado Springs, CO. 80995

Golf Traveler
2575 Vista Del Mar Dr.
Ventura, CA. 93001-3920

U.S. GOLF MAGAZINES

Golf World
5520 Park Ave.
Trumbull, CT. 06611

Senior Golfer
55 Corporate Dr.
Trumbull, CT. 06611

Golf For Women
Merideth Corp.
1716 Locust Street
Des Moines, IA. 50336

Women's Golf
5520 Park Ave.
P.O. Box 395
Trumbull, CT. 06611-0395

Golf Pro
Fairchild Magazines
7 West 34th St.
New York, NY. 10001

Pacific Northwest Golfer
155 N.E. 100th Street Suit 100
Seattle, WA. 98125

Great Lakes Golf
Gt Publications
P.O. Box 2493
Dearborn, MI. 48124

Inside Golf
Surfer Publications
33046 Cable Aviadar
San Juan Capistran, CA. 92675

Golf Georgia
121 Village Parkway Bldg 3
Maritta, GA. 30067

South Links
1040 William Hilton Parkway
P.O. Box 7628
Hilton Head Island, SC.. 29938

Golf Journal
USGA Golf House
P.O. Box 708
Far Hills, NJ. 07931-0708

Golf Illustrated
5300 City Plex Tower
2448 E.81st Street
Tulsa, OK. 74137

Golf Magazine
Times Mirror Magazines
2 Park Ave.
New York, NY. 10016-5675

The Golfer
42 W 38th Street
New York, NY. 10018-6210

Golf Tips
Werner Publishing Corp.
12121 Wilshire Blvd. #1220
Los Angeles, CA. 90025-1175

Golf Week
7657 Commerce Center Drive
Orlando, FL. 32819-8923

Fore Florida
1025 Sw Martin Downs Blvd # 200
Palm City, FL. 34990

Links
P.O. Box 7628
Hilton Head Island, SC. 29938

Golf News Magzine
P.O. Box 1040
Rancho Mirage, CA. 92270

Western Links
1040 William Hilton Parkway
P.O. Box 7628
Hilton Head Island, SC. 29938

Golf Shop Operations
5520 Park Ave.
Trumbull, CT. 06611

Titles Availble From SCHAEFER'S PUBLISHING

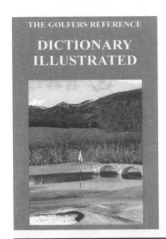

DICTIONARY ILLUSTRATED
Publication date: May 1999

WRITTEN BY: DUNCAN SWIFT

2000+ Terms and Phrases
300+ Illustrations
Golfers Resourses
    29 Golf Magazines
    130 International Golf Associations
    120 Men's Golf Associations
    110 Women's Golf Associations
    120 Junior's Golf Associations
ISBN: 0-9658132-1-5 LCCN: 98-89215
SIZE: 6x9 PAGES: 256 PAPERBACK
PRICE: US $16.95 / $21.95 CAN

GOLF GAMES AND SIDE BETS
Publication date: August 1999

WRITTEN BY: DUNCAN SWIFT

51 Side Bets
58 Twosome Games
42 Threesome Games
100 Foursome Games
116 Tournament Games
50 Charts
Handicap
Golf Rules and Relief
Indexed
ISBN: 0-9658132-3-1 LCCN: 98-83068
SIZE: 6x9 PAGES: 256 PAPERBACK
PRICE: US $16.95 / $ 21.95 CAN

MANUAL
Publication date: November 1999

WRITTEN BY: DUNCAN SWIFT

400+ Illustrations
30+ Charts
Etiquette
The Basics of Golf
The Clubs - Your Tools of the Trade
The Swing - How it is Done
Types of Iron and Wood Shots
Advanced Shots in Special Conditions
Corrections for Common Faults
Indexed
ISBN: 0-9658132-0-7 LCCN: 97-068575
SIZE: 6x9 PAGES: 256 PAPERBACK
PRICE: $16.95 / $ 21.95 CAN

ORDER FORM

QUANITY	TITLE	PRICE
_____	**DICTIONARY ILLUSTRATED**	_____
_____	**GOLF GAMES AND SIDE BETS**	_____
_____	**REFERENCE MANUAL**	_____

Michigan residents add 6% tax.   SUB. TOTAL   _____

Please allow 2-6 weeks delivery.   SHIP./HAND   _____

Please include $3.00 shipping and
handling for each book ordered.   MICH. TAX 6%   _____

U.S. Currency only.   TOTAL   _____

Name: _____

Address: _____

_____

_____

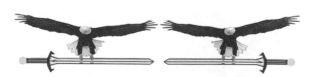

SCHAEFER'S PUBLISHING
P.O. Box 5544
Dearborn, MI. 48128-5544
schaed@idt.net

SCHAEFER'S PUBLISHING
P.o. Box 5544
Dearborn, Michigan
48128-5544
Email: schaed@idt.net

SPECIAL THANKS
To our Heavenly God who gives us the life
and the beautiful landscape to play on.
And to our Family and Friends for their
inspiration and support.